DEAR HENRIETTA,

I SINCERBLY HOPE
MY STORY HELPS YOU.
BE WELL!   KEN

It Takes Guts To Be Me

Editor: Ronda Del Boccio
Contact information:
Ken Jensen
Email: Ken@ItTakesGutsToBeMe.com
URL: http://www.ItTakesGutsToBeMe.com

Visit www.booksurge.com to order additional copies

KEN JENSEN

IT TAKES GUTS TO BE ME

HOW AN EX-MARINE BEAT BIPOLAR DISORDER

2008

It Takes Guts To Be Me

ACKNOWLEDGEMENTS

I sincerely thank Glenn Dietzel and his team at
www.AwakenTheAuthorWithin.com,
for helping me develop this book.

In specific, I thank Ronda Del Boccio at
www.Storyation.com,
John Hollingsworth, Darrell Wingerak, and Glenn himself for making this
whole thing possible. I could never have done this without your guidance.

You fine people showed me what I could do.

-For My Parents-
You Never Left My Side, Ever.
I Owe You Everything.
I Love You Both.

-And To 990-
I'll Never Have Friends More Loyal Than You Guys.
We Were Young And We Were Marines.
Semper Fi!
Lou Rawls!

INTRODUCTION

JOIN ME IN MY HEAD A MOMENT, WON'T YOU?

OK, here's the deal real quick: You have bipolar disorder or you are a friend or family member trying to help a loved one who has bipolar disorder. Either way, life sucks. We can be clear on that one part, correct? I thought so.

I searched, mostly in vain, for about six of the eight years I got my ass handed to me by bipolar disorder. I did find the answers I so desperately needed but c'mon...SIX years!

And life was hairy and scary while I searched. Depression, isolation, dissociation, and fear were constant backseat drivers in my ride down Insane Lane. My aim is to help you skip all the legwork I already put in. I turned myself into a research machine to find the help I honestly thought might not actually exist.

But it does and it is in this book. Please read my story so you will believe that I walk my talk.

My life has been pretty damned harsh so much of the language in this book is the same. If you are an overly sensitive soul, you are not going to be comfortable. I'm just getting my point across and telling the tales as they happened.

My Marine Corps years figured heavily into shaping my mental health and all my perspectives on life. I went into the Corps a might unstable and came out pretty much deranged. I do not blame the Corps. The Marine lifestyle and perspectives simply make it easy for one such as myself to flourish in all the wrong ways. The Corps didn't see me coming. Shit, I didn't see me coming.

I used to be someone who scared the crap out of people with my presence alone. I didn't actually have to do anything to make them start worrying. The potential for wrong just poured off of me. I don't miss that guy.

If I don't show you how I became sick, why I was sick, why I chose the steps for recovery that I did, how they work, how I see life now, and why it is better and achievable; if I just *hand* you the steps—you won't appreciate them for what they're worth, you won't understand why I chose them, you won't believe what I say, and ultimately, you won't act on them, thereby saving yourself. You'll not only stay sick, you'll add unnecessary frustration to your life thinking yet one more person has deceived you in your search for relief. The Internet and self-help aisles of your local bookstore are swarming with charlatans out to make a quick buck and half-assed systems developed by others who I don't think were ever a fraction as sick as I was. I don't share what I *think*—I share what I *know* from <u>direct personal experience</u>.

My way is not the only way but it is sensible, scientific, measurable, and it worked for me, a guy who was very close to prison, total insanity, or death. Very close.

Half of this book covers my Marine Corps years. Just becoming a Marine changes you for life. Now take that and add to it the destructive personal perspectives I held and you'll see why the Marine years figure so heavily into all that I am still.

I have moved on in life. I left the Marines in '91. I am no warmonger. I don't want to hurt anyone. I really do wish the whole damn world would just get along. But it won't and that's why there are Marines and the training they put in me eternally lies just beneath the surface. There is no shaking it. The difference is I choose to use these skills in a friendlier, constructive manner today. So I had to share much about my time in the Corps. It was, and in many ways still is, who I am.

I had a hellacious fight with multiple drugs and drinking. Although I don't address that stuff big time in this particular book, you may recognize yourself in me and that should give you hope because I got rid of it all.

If your life is not working and you are drinking or doing drugs but can't see the wrong in that? Well, your problem is bigger than just mental illness and I don't have room to address both in one book.

The thing I'd like you to know the most is this: I remember the pain and despair and I wish to help you free yourself from it just as I did.

Read on!

IN THE BEGINNING…

KEN JENSEN

THE NUCLEAR FAMILY. REALLY NUCLEAR

Out of respect to my parents, both of whom I love dearly, I am only going over the highlights of my youth. They both played very specific roles in creating who I became, both good and bad. Nobody needs to know all the specifics. Plus, who among us hasn't had a shitty childhood or at least wished some things went better than they did?

My Dad taught me how to work hard, how to do things right the first time, how to treat people properly, a love of the outdoors, and how to drink.

My Mom taught me how much a parent can love her children, that you should go to any length to support your children, and unfortunately, what the bleak world of madness is all about.

I am happy to say that I still learn from both of them actively today and the negative traits they showed me when I was young have long since vanished. They are my foundation and my strength as I came to rely on them far more in my adult life than I ever did as a child. But growing up had some pretty bad spots.

I was beat and hit a lot as a kid almost exclusively by my mother. As I got older, I learned from my Dad that drinking made everything better and could turn a good time into a great time. He didn't actively train me in this. I just watched and learned. He was a happy man and this was only magnified when he drank.

Everybody loved partying with my father. I realized this and began seriously looking into it around the time I turned 15.

Everybody loved my Mom in general. She had her public persona and her family one. They didn't always match too well. Later in life many people were surprised and still are at times to learn that my mom went through some very unhappy times as a person and wasn't too proud of her mothering duties either. Family secrets and public masks. So it went.

My Dad didn't realize until much later that even though drinking was a lot of fun and he was not a mean drunk, he gave up too much of his life to it. Time he could have spent with his family. He knows he helped my brother and I to develop views on drinking that would come to hurt the whole family quite a bit.

My brother went down most of the same dark paths I did. He put his own personal spin on things. We weren't exactly alike and he never really seemed to tear the ass out of life as intensely as I did. But he filled a number of statistical columns in impressive fashion for quite a while.

My poor Ma had misdiagnosed mental problems. She developed many physical ailments over time. Depression and stress were always huge on her to do list. In an attempt to treat all her ills she was over-medicated by the different doctors she visited. They weren't communicating and she faithfully took all her pills because that's how it worked. Doctor gives you a pill-you must need it right? It's a wonder she survived what they did to her. She then took all that mess and passed it on to me. Not her fault. Wasn't right what she did to me but not her fault.

We did have nice times as a family. However, for the purposes of this book I'm just shedding light on the foundations of my future bipolar disorder. It wasn't all Hell though. Just a constant state of dis-ease and varying amounts of chaos. I did figure out that things in my house were not the same in most of the other kids'. Not that I knew of, anyway. There were a few other fun families that were similar in dysfunction to ours but I sort of grew up in happy land here in the woods of upstate New York. Most kids' stories were not as dramatic as mine was.

For different reasons, I was quasi-ostracized growing up. I spent a lot of time alone in the woods. Nothing bad ever happened to me there. About half my life was spent climbing trees. I loved climbing! When I got a little older, we had snowmobiles and dirt bikes and I swam in lakes and streams, my whole life. So I was in pretty good shape at least.

Ken's note: I've never fit in anywhere my whole life and I wasn't safe at home. When you're like this, you find others like you, and they are just as maligned, usually. So the roots of my illness were formed from this isolation, lack of a safe haven, very little support from parents, physical abuse, and honing all the wrong life skills with others like me. This was how my bipolar was born. One of my steps specifically addresses all of this.

OK—JUST ONE MORE QUART

In my 15th summer, I started sneaking drinks with a friend I'd made in another town where I'd go swimming. It was a lot of fun. But we had a little accident one day. We had access to gallons of vodka. We made some really big cocktails and had a chugalug contest. This did two things. It made us drunk enough to make very bad decisions and it anesthetized us making it easier to drink even more, fast. We were too drunk and too numb to realize what we were doing to ourselves next.

I blacked out right after that first big mug. It wasn't very long after, probably less than half an hour, when I drank most of a gallon of vodka, pretty much straight. I'm assuming it was a show of manhood kind of thing.

I legally/technically died a handful of times in the back of the ambulance and again in the ICU. I was in a coma for a certain amount of hours and I did in fact have a near death experience (or, DURING death depending on your point of view). I was in an all black place. Sorry, no light, no tunnel, just shades of black. I don't know how I could see but I could. I was in a void, suspended on a footbridge made of black clouds. I felt a sense of infinite depth of space above and below me. I was headed somewhere but I don't know where. All around me was clouds, black clouds. I knew I was dead. It was a rock solid fact to me. I was also at peace, a profound calm. I was happy that I was dead and I didn't want to go back. Dead was fine with me.

I wasn't thinking about how death should be either. I was simply experiencing being dead. That's it. Obviously, I came back but I don't remember leaving whatever place that was. I should point out that I wasn't suicidal either. Self-destructive and unhappy at times but I didn't want to die. As far as that goes, we were on our way for a day at the creek. That was my happiest place in the whole world! No. We were just young and stupid and suffered from a distinct lack of foresight.

Ken's note: Alcohol is the fluid that flows in Satan's veins for some of us. (I'm being metaphorical, not religious, here.) It ruined me many times over. It took me to low points I'll never fully disclose. My bipolar was reinforced by drinking and later in life, drinking helped it blossom into a pain that only Shakespeare could fully do justice. Alcoholics Anonymous is good stuff and can help. But the bipolar part of you can make it impossible to sit through meetings or open up to another. Let me help you deal with the mind and as you improve, you'll be able to maintain your sobriety if this is you.

KEN JENSEN

I WANT YOU! TO GET OUT OF MY HOUSE!

I hated all my school years and my close friends all lived in other towns. I was the kid who wore the army fatigue shirts. I skipped school constantly in the 11th grade usually to drink. Drinking was an escape but it also made me feel like a man. My tolerance was huge. I could out drink just about anybody without passing out. I drew strength from that. Plus, drinking was just damn fun back then!

There came a time when I'd screwed up somehow to where it got back to my parents. I was 17. Dad took me out on the back porch and laid it all out for me.

"Get a new hobby or get a new home."

Succinct but potent. He wasn't gonna tolerate me just drinking and doing whatever I wanted while living under his roof. You know the speech. Then he outlined The New Plan.

"You don't want to go to college and we can't afford to send you anyway. There's no work in this town and you have no skills. Your only chance to have a life is to join the Service."

Dad had been in the Army Reserves for quite a while by that time so here's how he saw it:

"You're not joining the Army because I've been in it a long time and it's all fucked up. If you come home wearing a dog dish and bell-bottoms I'll disown you at the door. That leaves you two choices: You can go the hard way or the easy way, Marines or Air Force. I don't care which but pick one."

Well, I was no hero. I picked easy. I even convinced a friend to join with me. We were gonna be bestest friends forever. Unfortunately, the air force recruiter was not in all three times we went to meet him. We were becoming frustrated. I bumped into my friend at school one day and he casually informed me that he'd joined the Army. I was pissed! Said he got tired of waiting. This violated the terms of our friendship as far as I was concerned.

So, I said, "Well fuck you then. Tom's going into the Marines. I'll go with him."

Ba dump bump! That's how one of the most critical decisions of my entire life was made.

THE DAWN OF A NEW DAY:
THE MARINE CORPS YEARS

YOU GOTTA REALLY GET DOWN IN THERE

I breezed through boot camp. I was in great shape before I ever got there so the physical portions of training were a snap. The head games were easy enough to tolerate over time. There was one event, which took place during my training, that is particularly germane to my story. It was brief but contained the spark of all I was to become while in the Marines.

We were living in the field for a week practicing war game type stuff. We received a visit from a Captain. One by one we were brought before him at a little table set up in the woods. He simply wanted to know why we joined the Marines.

"Well, sir, I have been getting in trouble because of drinking and I hope the Marines will teach me how to be disciplined enough to stay out of trouble."

He smiled ever so slightly but maintained his professional veneer.

"Well, young man, the Marines have been known to do a little bit of drinking on the whole so you might want to be careful with that."

Prophetic little exchange that turned out to be. You'll see.

I graduated and got one month's leave. When it was time for me to go to my first base, I became very angry and dejected. I didn't want to go. I had never given full thought to what my five-year contract meant. It was all kind of a game up 'til then. I couldn't see past making it through boot camp. The reality of my situation started sinking in. I got on the plane with a heavy heart.

My first base was in Tennessee. I was there for my first school. I learned that I still wasn't really considered a Marine and wouldn't be until I was in the Fleet doing my job. That would turn out to be a full year later. So, at this base we were treated like kids. We called it "Fourth Phase Boot Camp." There were three phases on Parris Island so this was the fourth.

Here's a fine example of the ridiculousness I encountered in my very first week. In the middle of my first field day, I came upon a guy hammering a plastic handled bowl brush down into the plumbing of a shitter in the community head. He was literally using a large book as a hammer.

"What the hell is he doing?" I asked someone nearby.

"We have to get the brush as far into the trap as possible. Then we put a stick though that wire on the end and rotate it. That gets all the shit out. The Sgt. Major inspects the barracks himself. He's a skinny fucker. He'll get down on his knees and force his arm down into the trap, then he'll scrape the pipe with his fingernails. If he finds any shit under his nails, the whole barracks fails and we have to reclean everything."

This guy was serious!

"Fuck that!" I said. "If he wants to find shit that bad then I wish him the best of luck. What the fuck!?"

Welcome to the Marines.

I handled this part of life worse than most around me. I was already a drunk and I believe this time is when my mind started cracking.

I experienced my first epiphany. I was walking to the E-Club to get drunk. In Tennessee, it was legal to drink at 18 if you were in uniform. This made it too easy for me to achieve self-destruction. I was thinking hard about how fucked up my life had become. As far as I knew, the way life was on this base was how it was going to be for my entire enlistment. I didn't know any better at the time. Then it dawned on me that I had four and three quarter more years of this bullshit. It was as if the sky cracked open above me when I realized this. The instantaneous crushing weight of despair almost drove me insane on the spot. It hit me so hard as to defy proper description.

I could not tolerate the thought of living like this for almost five more years. Something bad in my mind clicked into place that very moment. I was irrevocably changed for the worse. Somehow, I got over it enough to continue on to the club where I then drank myself into oblivion.

Ken's note: Had there been full time war to occupy my hours, the entire length of my duty, I'd have been better off. It has taken me years to understand why I hated being enlisted the way I did. The major problem was boredom with no hope of escape combined with a spirit that knew, even back then, that there was much better waiting for me elsewhere.

I wanted more out of life and the Marines was too restrictive and constrictive. I felt like I was strangling the whole time I was in. Imagine a job you can't quit. Just can't. That's simply a lighter duty form of prison. When your mind is not free, you are effectively in prison.

None of this is news to anyone who's been in, but for a creative type personality, it is a horror.

I proceeded to fill my hours in all the wrong ways. I searched for escape, instead of growth. I committed mental suicide. I was a psychotic ghost while I served.

This brings to bear the importance of living the life you want and should be living. To not do so, brings on mental illness in varying degrees.

I help people figure out their purpose.

WELCOME TO THE MACHINE

O blivion and I got to know each other well during this time. I fell apart fast. Someone turned me in to the alcohol and drug division as someone with a potential drinking problem. Not an unreasonable assumption for someone to make but I was pissed nonetheless. I didn't think I had a drinking problem then. I was in denial. It's almost comical to look back and be aware of that now. You really are a different person under the influence. You operate with a different reality than all around you and you don't even know it. I very quickly learned how to beat the system. Maybe not beat it but I definitely learned there were parts of it that could be manipulated to my advantage.

There were three levels to the treatment program. Level One was a simple class attended at night for about a month and that was it. Level Two consisted of a couple months of part-time daily classes on every damn thing there is to know about drugs and drinking and mandatory AA meetings. This lasted 3 or 4 months, depending. Level Three was detox, hospital time. 45 days to dry out combined with counseling, classes, group, AA, the whole shebang. This lasted at least a year and sometimes more. If you were bad enough you could skip a level.

I got placed in Level One. I would end up going through Level One and Two twice. Normally you would progress to Level Three and if you fucked up again you were kicked out on a less than honorable discharge. We all avoided that like the plague.

Because of my constant traveling around the globe and some very deft bullshit slinging on my part (shoulda got an Oscar), my counseling records were never on hand or current when I'd get busted again. This is how I avoided ever going to detox and how I repeated the system. I don't think anyone else ever pulled that off. I needed help but I had no intention of ever quitting while I was in. I knew I couldn't do it.

Ken's note: Again, if you need to stop drinking (and you definitely have to if you're bipolar) AA is great but you might find it difficult. It is not the panacea of aid it's touted to be for some of us but they DO speak the truth at the meetings. I suggest you give it an attempt, here and there, just to educate yourself on this separate illness that is amplifying your bipolar illness. They're as dedicated to keeping you dry as I am to keeping you sane. The two are intertwined. Plus, you may like it.

But I found the meetings to be too depressing and too much of a rehash of what I already knew. It became redundant and time wasteful for me. I've stayed sober for 3+ years at this writing, without their help, but I don't think I'm in the majority and I do believe fully in everything they say. I just don't want to "keep it green." I want to evolve past it all. This is a personal choice.

TWO HEADS ARE NOT ALWAYS BETTER THAN ONE

A few months later, Tom and I, (the guy I had joined with), got busted together. The night had started out ok. We went to a beer bust at a local bar. For two hours, a mug of beer was only 10 cents. We managed to put down just over 70 beers in that two-hour span. I'm not exaggerating. We had engaged in a vicious head-butting competition with each other for the bulk of those two hours. Later that night I would learn that the one-inch thick mat of fluid extending from my hairline to my eyebrows was properly termed a "contusion of the skull." The MP's who arrested us were nice enough to take us for X-rays at the base hospital.

This whole night was too sad. We were literally at the front door of the barracks when Tom pin wheeled out of my grip and laughingly yelled something about tires. Tom's car tires were destroyed and he didn't have money to buy new ones. He did however know of a similar car in another unit's parking lot that had "free" tires on it. We just had to go liberate them from the car and we were set.

The following day I would learn that I had become an accessory to a theft. The cops surrounded us while we worked and we were so wasted we hadn't even heard them. I sure did have a lot of loaded weapons pointed at me that night. Suffice to say our tire hijacking failed. The next day I was sitting in an office receiving my official talking to.

The Staff Sgt. said, "Look. We both know you're a fuckup. You've had two drinking-related charges in less than 6 months and that's only for the stuff anyone's *aware* of. You're just gonna get worse. You know it and I know it. I have the power, right here and now, to start processing you out with a less than honorable if you want me to. Whattaya want to do? Ya want out?"

At that point, I was massively hung over with a crushing headache from the head butting. I knew he was right and every fiber in my being wanted out. He was handing me my greatest wish on a silver platter. Then I thought of the shame of returning home under those circumstances and told him no. It was the hardest thing I'd ever had to do. The car owner ended up dropping the charges but my record showed the offense anyway. I left Tennessee very soon after but Tom and I were on a different schedule. We got split up and I wouldn't see him for a few more months.

KEN JENSEN

WELCOME TO FLORIDA—CLIMB OUR MAJESTIC HOTELS

I had a short stay in Cecil Field, Florida. I first tried checking in at the Marine base across the road from the navy base I was supposed to be at. It took me all night to find out where I was supposed to check in but I eventually found it. This was to be the first of many transient barracks I would stay at over the years. Transient barracks, I would learn, roughly translated to "shithole" in the Marines. What a dump. I was only in there for a couple of weeks. Got hammered a few times but managed to stay out of trouble. I didn't work on anything while I was there, just waited for orders to my next base.

I got sent to NAS Jacksonville, a huge naval base in Florida. The barracks were in bad shape but life was good there. We had maid service for a dollar a day and we were allowed to drink in the barracks. Navy rules. I took advantage of that as much as possible over the next couple of months.

I wasn't too happy here either but school was mellower and I did fit in a trip to Daytona Beach for Spring Break. The things I saw! And did! I witnessed live sex shows in hotel rooms. I evaded cops by scaling a hotel exterior up to the fifth floor before I found an open window. I don't even recall what I'd done to make them chase me but I'm sure it was warranted.

I met a heroin addict and went on a run with him to get another fix just to see what that might look like. I saw kids doing beer bongs from 10th floor balconies down to the beach below.

I spent a sleepless night in a room with some guys who were setting off firecrackers in the ears of their passed out friends. I watched a guy try to outrun the cops in his car but get stuck on the beach. The cops piled out and beat him mercilessly while dozens of us watched.

I was a spectator for a two-man power barfing contest. Their goal? To get as much slop into the seats of someone's brand new convertible parked below with its roof down. There was much more but those were the highlights. All in just two and a half days.

Ken's note: This is the flow to my whole time in the Marines. I partied all that I could and behaved outrageously all that I could. I had a lot of fun but more often, I was lost, miserable, and hung over. My drinking rapidly went from "partying" to "unbridled alcoholism." It just was what I did. It was a form of insanity. It destroyed me. I am grateful in the most powerful sense that I am sober today. I don't miss it. I crave it sometimes but I don't miss it. That, in itself, is a blessing.

LIFE'S A BEACH

I went to Beaufort, SC next. It was here that I was supposed to now practice fixing the gear I'd been trained on. That never happened. The senior Marines mostly used us for the dirty jobs they didn't want to do. However, there was a benefit to being stationed here. Hilton Head Island was only a stone's throw from the base. It was a big resort area that was home to families on vacation with their young daughters. A lot happened on that beach. My group managed to stay perpetually drunk for almost two months.

I remember our Barracks Sgt. telling us, "You guys keep drinking like this and you're gonna die. Do you even realize what you're doing to yourselves? How bad you look?"

Nope. We didn't. And we didn't care.

We virtually lived on the beach. Almost every night after work we'd drive to the beach, party all night, sleep on the beach into the morning, then return to the base for work that afternoon. It was a paradise, everyone young and drunk, no cops, and plenty of girls.

Tons of public sex at night. Nothing was forbidden. I met the girl of my dreams on that beach. I only had her for two weeks but it was two of the best weeks of my life.

Through a fluke, I got 21 days travel time to get to my next base. It was only a plane ride away and I was confused. The Corporal at S-1 made it plainly clear that he could give a shit about what my orders said and that I should quit questioning them and enjoy the vacation. So I did.

I checked out of Beaufort but stayed on the beach. I'd ride back to base once in a while for a shower and some food but I basically stayed on the beach. I was calling home one day and found out an uncle had died so I had to go home for the funeral. That was a painful scene. My uncle was very much loved by all. I was home for a bit then moved on.

HAVE SOME COKE AND A SMILE

Camp Pendleton, CA. Another transient barracks. These were in better shape though. I was only here while I waited for a bird to Japan where I was to stay for a year. It was here that I ran into an old friend from Tennessee.

Dennis was a few years older than the rest of us and he'd been given the choice between jail and the Marines by a judge. Some sort of real estate deal gone awry. He was loud, psychotic, had the energy of ten men, and had a big eagle tattooed on his shoulder. He had a way of laughing maniacally that told you "I think that's funny but I want to kill something and I don't know why." He was magic. We fed on each other's violent tendencies and we seemed to see everything the same way.

My time with him in Tennessee was probably when my back problems started. We liked to pick each other up and run down the hall full bore into the concrete wall using the other guy's back as a ram.

A mistake was made and I received a double paycheck at the time. It amounted to a whole $520 but I felt rich! I told Dennis and he instantly formed a plan.

"Ever do coke?" he asked.

I said no but that I was up for it. Turned out he used to live somewhere nearby. That weekend we went to a local car rental joint and paid for the only car left on the lot; a purple Monte Carlo that had seen better days. It was perfect! We headed north, scored some blow, and set out for Great Adventure, the theme park. I was a little scared about snorting coke but Dennis talked me through it fine. It was a sunny day. We were cruising along at about 95 mph, radio blasting and doing lines off the back of the car ashtray, the only thing we could find with a smooth surface. It was classic.

We made it to the park but found it to be mighty inconvenient to have to wait on line so long in between snorts. We soon left. Around 3 am, we ran out of snow and I was introduced to the fantabulous world of jonesing. I never craved anything like I did that next nonexistent line. We simply sat in the car doing nothing in the parking lot of a convenience mart waiting for beer to go back on sale in the morning. Sucked. I would not do coke for over three years after that.

Interesting side note: Upon checking in at the barracks, we were led through a most unique indoc. The Sgt. of the Barracks specifically told us he would not tolerate any defecation in a non-defecating area. He also said that Marines giving other Marines "Golden Showers" was expressly forbidden. No further explanation. I was shocked! What the hell was he talking about? I would soon find out.

We were in an open squad bay. One big room. I awoke one night to the screaming and hollering of a man in distress. I ran down to see the action. This one guy was passed out drunk in the top bunk and pissing himself. The screams were coming from the guy in the bottom bunk who had urine raining down on him from above. Sweet!

Some days after the coke weekend, Dennis came up to me in the barracks. He was very flustered about something. Not an unusual condition for him but this was more pronounced than normal. He had gone into the laundry room to do a load of wash and found a guy with his pants down shitting into the top of an open washer. Dennis flipped out and asked the guy, "What the *hell* are you doing?!" He found the drunken response to be less than adequate but he was too disgusted to even bother searching for a better answer. He punched the guy in the face, knocking him out and then stayed with his machine until his wash was done.

But now he was in front of me asking, "What the fuck is wrong with this place man?!"

I couldn't do much more than laugh. He was one of the few guys I knew who made getting all pissed off look so comical.

WELCOME TO THE SUCK

I caught a bird out of LAX to Iwakuni. We drank all the booze on the plane. It was a 21-hour flight. We'd had enough time to get wasted, pretty much take over the plane, pass out, and experience a hangover all on the same trip. There were 19 of us. What a mess we were.

When we arrived in Osaka, nobody was waiting for us. We slept on our piled up sea bags on the sidewalk outside the terminal for most of the night. They wouldn't let us stay inside. Thank God it was August.

Later, we secured some rooms at a nice hotel. About 12 hours after arrival somebody came and got us.

Spent another fantastic weekend in another transient barracks. This one was condemned but we got put in it anyway. Stank like a cave. We learned right away that we had to shower fast. If we took too long, raw sewage backed up from out of the drains. The barracks I got permanently placed in were condemned too but in better condition.

Iwakuni is where I finally entered the Fleet. I was officially in the Suck. This term was derived from "Fuck the Suck," a colloquialism for being enlisted. Never knew where you might come across "FTS" written or scratched on a piece of equipment.

I never did get to work on the equipment I was trained to fix. I ended up going to work center 990. We were the maintenance shop for the Mobile Maintenance Facilities. These were climate-controlled containers that mostly avionics guys worked in. They repaired parts off the jets. I was like the building super for the "vans" as we called them. I kept them hot or cold, managed their power supply, and moved the containers with heavy equipment whenever they had to go somewhere else.

I didn't figure out until much later that my shop was staffed by mostly throwaways. We didn't officially exist in the Big Book, which listed every job there was in the Air Wing. My shop was actually considered an extra duty posting as we were made up mostly of guys on loan for 6 months from other shops.

We had our own little world in that Quonset hut in Japan. We had an emergency stash of vodka in a footlocker filled mostly with $2 a bottle rotgut. Anybody was free to dip into the supply if they were broke and just had to get drunk. The only rule was to replace what you used on payday. We were tucked out of the way and were left to our own devices. We rarely got an unwanted visit. I felt we were unique to the rest of the unit.

We had many hundreds of vans to maintain. Our job was half-technical and half physical. On the physical days we busted our asses. We handled many hundreds of individual doors weighing 30 to 70 pounds apiece. We dragged or carried hundreds of power cables weighing from 30 to 250 pounds apiece. Butting kits (50-pound aluminum frames with padded material connecting them to form weatherproof walkways between two vans) had to be installed or removed. Dunnage (which was usually 4X4 lumber in 10-foot lengths for the vans to rest upon) had to be laid in place or taken up and piled elsewhere and if heavy equipment was not available, we even had ways of moving the vans themselves by hand. The vans weighed anywhere from 6000 pounds up to 30,000 pounds but most were around 10 to 15 thousand pounds. Often, generators had to be manhandled into position. These were on wheels but weighed 6000 pounds and were a bitch to move by hand. The big ones were 11,000 pounds and we moved those with heavy equipment.

Hooking up the cables was even worse. Hours of pain, frustration, and questioning your place in the Universe. Various components would sometimes be warped or misaligned and would not go into place as we needed them to without a lot of bleeding, sweating, and copious amounts of swearing.

It was interesting work, especially when a large move took place. Most everything was indeed moved by hand. We froze in the winter, cooked in the summer, and busted our backs all year round.

Right outside of base there were about 20 or 30 bars. Our money wasn't worth much out in town as the Japanese economy was much stronger than ours was. But drinking on base was cheap. Six packs of Bud often went on sale for two dollars each. A fifth of good scotch—$6 or $7.

We'd preflight on base. We borrowed the term from when a plane is checked out before takeoff. Then we'd head out to town, already drunk and not have to spend a lot of money to stay that way. There were drinks out in town with ingredients not even legal for sale in the States. One of my favorites was "Snake Juice": poisonous snake in a bottle of Saki. Very expensive and high chaos potential after consumption.

While in Iwakuni, we took getting wasted to a whole new level. Much too much happened during this time to recount it all but heavy drinking was always involved.

Ken's note: My time in Iwakuni and Yechon shaped me in ways that lingered until my early thirties. Some of it was magical. Most of it was hurtful. I had to fight hard to stop thinking from this perspective. This era was that potent to my formation as an adult.

You are doing the same thing in some fashion. You can break free, as I did.

THE NIGHTTIME, SNIFFLING, SNEEZING, COUGHING, "HOW THE HELL DID I GET ON THE MOON?" COUGH MEDICINE

It was during this time that I was introduced to "Robing." We'd chugalug a 4 oz' bottle of Robitussin DM and trip our faces off. The cough suppressant created an LSD-like effect. Matter of fact we used to call it "poor man's acid."

How horrible it was to choke down though. So many guys did it that the stuff was hard to keep on the shelves. I knew guys who could drink 4 to 15 bottles in a day and somehow live. Swore they enjoyed it.

One unit in particular was famous for having Robe parties whenever a new shipment arrived at the PX. They'd just buy it all.

Robing was a last ditch kind of thing with me. It was the grossest thing I would ever do to my body. It took me years to discover that I didn't even enjoy it. It would trash me so bad that I would never remember how bad it made me feel overall. That's pretty trashed.

Ken's note: Don't Robe. Ever. You pay for it in a way you'd never understand until it was too late. You see a world best left alone. Trust me.

KEN JENSEN

CAN'T A MAN JUST SCREAM AT HIS FOOD IN PEACE?

I picked up another drinking-related charge at this time too, public drunkenness. I was at a little restaurant called Snack Superman. Kept passing out face-first in my plate of chicken then waking up to scream various obscenities then passing out again. Not too creative I know, but enough so to get me in trouble. Somehow I avoided treatment this time around. But I was punished.

I was at my "office hours." It was a way to be punished informally to avoid any possible brig time you might get awarded at a court martial. The Colonel was pissed. Purple in the face pissed. My boss was there as well.

"What are we going to do with this young Marine, Staff Sgt.?" the Colonel asked.

"Leave that up to me sir. I have just the thing."

Hiram sounded extremely pissed as well. I was shaking in my boots. I thought we were cool with each other. We were dismissed and Hiram slammed the door behind us. I was a dead man.

Once outside he said, "Goddam Jensen! What did you do?" But his tone of voice was softer.

"I don't have anything to do to you. What are we gonna do?"

He had been acting the whole time to get the Colonel off my back. I was so relieved!

This became my punishment: A big exercise was coming up for Korea and we needed extra power distribution boxes to be built. We had to build them ourselves. So every day after work, I went to supper and then reported back to the shop. Once there, I'd meet three other guys who had already purchased many cases of beer and we would spend the night drinking and building these boxes. It took all of us to get it done on time. That was my punishment. Ooh-rah!

Ken's note: You can't get arrested and/or detained as much as I did and not have it affect you for the worse. I share most of my arrests so that you can see what I put myself through and how close I came to prison.

As of now, I have no more legal rope. I pull anything, I go to prison. And that's where I'll die. I can't do prison. I'm not that tough. I can admit it. And my mind will not tolerate the imprisonment. I will go insane and die from it or piss off the wrong guy while I'm insane and he'll free me. Nope. I go out of my way to behave now.

KEN JENSEN

YOU'RE NOT DRUNK 'TIL YOU'RE BLIND DRUNK

A few weeks later, I went to Yechon, Korea. I lived in a 12-man tent for five months through the winter and into the summer. So much happened in Korea it's unreal.

I tried acid for the first time. That was phenomenal. I'd be lying if I said I regretted it. The man to introduce me to it was my boss. He was heavily into white and black magic and his ultimate goal in life was to learn how to become a shape shifter. You know, change into a cat or a bird at will. I had some extremely interesting conversations with him whether we were tripping or not.

Found a new drink to look into as well. Saki with formaldehyde mixed in it. It was called Soju. The locals drank it all the time. We liked it because it allowed you to get totally shit faced drunk but still be able to perform sex.

Drinking Soju was equivalent to playing Russian roulette. We started hearing rumors of guys losing feeling in their limbs and being medevacced out to hospitals for treatment. One squadron leader made it illegal for his men to drink it. Seemed to cause a lot of fights too. I quit drinking it for a different reason.

I specifically drank nothing but soju one night just to see what would happen. The next morning when I woke up in my tent everything was black. I was confused because I could hear everybody getting ready for work. It was winter and I knew the propane stoves were burning. Plus we had two lights in the tent. I saw nothing. Nothing at all. It was terrifying.

After 10 frantic minutes I detected a pinhole of light. Over the next 15, I fully regained my sight. That little episode freaked us all out, me most of all. I never drank soju again and I don't think anyone else in my tent did either.

There was lots of sex to be had in Yechon. I racked up 19 girls, some more than once, in five months. I was in a friendly competition with a tent mate. It was based on the honor system.

When one of us returned to the tent in the morning it automatically meant we had spent the night out in town. All eyes would be on us as we entered the tent. We'd make a big show of leaning over the wooden card table and adding the new name to the list. Then everyone would cheer and the heat would be on the opposing player. He now had to score a long time to catch up. Scads of family fun this was!

KEN JENSEN

THE LOWEST PRICES IN TOWN!

I even helped initiate an official US government boycott. I was sitting outside of the beer tent on base and my CO was across from me, the same Colonel who I'd stood before at my last office hours. Overseas it was much more common to find officers and enlisted men hanging out together. Normally verboten. He was angry drunk.

"What the fuck are YOU lookin' at Marine?"

"Nothin' sir. Just enjoying my beer and the sun."

He relaxed and asked me how things were going.

"Could be better, sir. Ever since the units all rotated, the girls raised their rates in town. I've been here since the beginning of the operation so I know better. But the new guys don't know it and they're paying the higher amounts. We're getting hosed out there."

"Is that right? Well, we'll just see about that shit."

I didn't think anymore about it. But the next day we had a unit formation. The Colonel informed us that he had been made aware of the higher rates and that this was not correct. So liberty was rescinded until further notice. We were the main source of income for the town so in effect we closed the town.

Three days later we had another muster. Liberty was back on. I headed out to the Ville that night and learned that the rates were all back to normal. It always cracked me up that I initiated the official boycotting of a town based on hooker's rates.

I returned to Iwakuni for about a month and then I went back to the States for the first time in a year.

Ken's note: I mention the sex because, well, civilians just have no idea how the military operates in a third world country. There was an established health system for prostitutes run by the Navy to keep us healthy. And being "all the man you can be" was the highest priority at all times in the earlier years.

There's another reason. Sexual promiscuity, although a sporting art form in the military, indicates a bigger problem underneath.

Many young guys especially, want to get all the action they can, just due to hormones and peer pressure. But for me, this time established a rather dark part of me when it came to women. Nothing violent but rather, a twisted precedent was set in place that stuck with me right up until my mid thirties.

Sex becomes a way to validate yourself. Nothing new there but it can't really accomplish what the bipolar part of you wants it to. But you keep trying, just like when drinking or drugging, you keep trying to gain something that's not to be had.

I get more into this later. But for this time period, I hated the pressure of always appearing to be on the attack in proper manly fashion. I wasn't free to just be and maybe find a chick in some natural, healthier way. This will sound weird but the stress of constantly having to get laid was almost more than I could handle. And only in looking back can I see most of this was only in my own head.

We think our way into sickness, too. My system has a tool to fix that.

THE MARINE CORPS' REDHEADED STEP-SONS

E l Toro, California. This was now my Mother Base. I met the nucleus of who would become my lifelong best friends. They were different from anyone I'd yet encountered. They partied just as hard as me but were a more open-minded imaginative bunch. They moved me up a few notches from my rather narrow point of view.

I was locked in the overseas mindset, which is very different from life in the States. I don't mean just culturally. The whole military is different overseas than it is at home. You can get away with more and at different times life is more barbaric. So that's where my head was at when I met these guys. They helped me to begin thinking bigger.

I learned that the uniqueness of 990 was even more pronounced in El Toro. Our boss was a big drinker and very easy going. We had a lot of fun with him. He even let me and another Marine go north to see the Space Shuttle landing in the middle of the week. He felt it was important for two young guys to witness that.

I saved his ass one night while on call. I got word that I was needed at the flight line. Vans had arrived and nobody was claiming them but it was our kind of gear so we were picked to do something about it. I got a few guys together. We all had a few cocktails in us but were ok. There was a lot of brass standing around. High-level officers. My boss, the Gunny, met me. He was carrying his ever-present beer stein that he drank coffee from. He had his sunglasses on even though it was 10 pm. He was frantic.

"Jensen. Please tell me you have this under control!"

"I got it boss. Why the stress?"

He was wasted.

"They called me at my goddam bar in town!"

He actually had the number for his bar entered as a notification contact if he was needed.

"I'm too fucked up for this. Make me look good."

And I did. It was no sweat to do what was required and I was only buzzed. I always found that entire night to have been quite amusing.

We had around 1,000 vans here. We also had a bigger shop and more guys. Over the next three years many workers and many bosses would pass through our doors. We ran the shop the way we wanted. We got away with a lot. We also managed to get in trouble a lot both as a group and individually.

Some years later I ran into that first Gunny. I told him we missed having him as a boss and asked if he'd consider coming back to us.

"Fuck—that!" he said. "I used up 16 years of favors in 6 months keeping all you motherfuckers out of jail and convincing colonels not to bust your asses on the spot for different things you pulled! I ain't ever going back to that shop! You guys are crazy!"

He meant it. But I know he loved us or he wouldn't have burned up all the favors.

We lived under an odd dichotomy in 990. We partied too much. We fought any and all authority every chance we could. We never followed orders if we disagreed and if we were forced to do something we found some other way to get even. We didn't really do anything like the rest of the Marine Corps.

But we excelled at our job. That was the dichotomy. It was what always saved us. We always took great pride in our work. We worked harder than most of the guys who used our equipment and that made us feel superior to them. We always made sure that when it came to the job nobody could say nothin'.

There was no official training to do what we did so if we didn't do it it's not like someone could just step in and take our place. The job just encompassed too many areas. Even if someone could figure out one part, they weren't going to get it all. That gave us leverage. We were pretty much the reincarnation of the Black Sheep Squadron, just different toys. And we got off on that fact!

Whenever one of us got caught doing something minor we could usually get off by simply saying this phrase: "I'm 990." That's it. That would usually be enough for the higher-ranking asshole to just step away. Over time nobody really messed with us much. I guess they knew it would be a futile pursuit. If someone did press us on something we'd find a way to spin it in our favor or deny them what they wanted, even our own bosses.

Case in point: I was working on a Staff Sgt.'s air conditioner in a heat wave. He happened to be in charge of making sure any rules dealing with working life were followed. Quality Control, Quality Assurance, something like that. We simply referred to these guys as "The Gestapo." If life could be made unnecessarily harder, they would find that way and enforce it.

As I'm working, the Staff Sgt. shows up behind me to watch. In my effort to troubleshoot the air conditioner I was jumping two low voltage connections by sticking the end of a screwdriver between them.

Here's how bad these guys were:

"Marine? Is that the proper usage of that tool?"

"No Staff (You could get away with informally using Staff without the Sgt. part in some situations, usually with friends. It was also an indirect way of displaying a lack of respect to guys like this one.) but it's only 27 volts. I could stick my tongue in there. It ain't gonna hurt anything."

"The proper tool is two alligator clips connected by insulated wire. Are you using the correct tool?"

For a brief moment I became enraged. I couldn't believe this dickhead was fucking with me over this nothing issue. On top of it there's a heat wave taking place and it's HIS a/c I'm trying to get going! Then the full scope of the situation hit me and I instantly calmed down.

"No Staff Sgt. this is not the correct tool for the job. However, I know we don't possess the proper tool in our tool room and I will have to order it. I'll let you know when it comes in."

I was all smiles. I returned to my shop and told everyone that no one was to fix that a/c without speaking to me first. If we got any calls on it, there would ALWAYS be a higher priority job taking place and we would get to it when we could. I warned all my underlings that I'd kick the shit out of them if they fixed it behind my back. I wasn't joking.

I made that motherfucker sweat for two weeks in his box. I heard it could get up to 180 degrees inside a van in the summer if the air was out. I didn't fix that a/c until the Colonel ordered me to. But he did laugh when I told him the actual details.

"Son, you're too much. Fix his damn air conditioner so I don't have to listen to him whine anymore." He was laughing as he told me this.

I did shit like that for years. I never could see the sense in pissing off the guy who fixed the hot and cold. Now, we couldn't get away with absolutely everything but I guarantee we got away with more than anybody else did.

Ken's note: My personality began to alter at this stage. My new friends opened my mind to life in good ways, truly, but I also sunk farther into the bad thing I was becoming. I started packing on muscle, too.

Life at this base just started turning me into something slightly different for many reasons. It was me that was doing the changing but things were here that made it unavoidable.

AND THE GOOD NEWS KEEPS ROLLIN' IN

My second family tragedy occurred around now. I'm in my room and I'm hung over from the night before. I am wearing my underwear, one sock, and a T-shirt I got in Korea, which has Garfield smirking on the front. The caption above him reads, "I hate this fucking place."

There's a knock at the door. I open it to see a Major in his Charlies, ribbons and all. I instantly shit my pants but then I notice the clergyman brass on his one collar. It's the chaplain. So I know I'm not in trouble but there is some bad news coming nonetheless.

He sort of takes a glance at me but seems nonjudgmental.

"You'd better take a seat son. I have something hard to tell you."

Then he informs me of my Godparents' deaths.

I am nonplussed. Not out of callousness. It just seems somehow appropriate in my fucked up little world and I tell him so. He lingers a moment then sees that I am not an emotional wreck. Having nothing more to say he leaves.

I no longer remember how that may have affected me. I was sad but as I said, one more thing. I'm sure that was logged in and caused me some sort of distress down the road. I loved my Godparents very much.

KEN JENSEN

PROOF POSITIVE THAT FAST FOOD IS BAD FOR YOUR HEALTH

Carl and I scored one for the books. This was some night. It began in the drive through at a fast food restaurant. We were wasted and waiting our turn. When the car in front moved up Carl was slow to close the gap. Someone honked their horn at us in protest for our lag time. Carl took this personal and jumped out of the truck to go talk to the rude individuals in question. I waited a minute or so but my hunger propelled me into action. I took over the driver's seat and attempted to move the truck forward. I misjudged the distance and hit the car in front of me. Now we had an incident to take care of.

I pulled away into the bigger parking lot to talk to the driver of the other car. Nice kid. We exchanged information and I promised we'd pay for the cosmetic damage I'd caused. No problem.

Somehow the situation degenerated from there. There was a large group of kids nearby and they were aware of what had happened. They were mad at us. One of them decided to fight Carl. The attacking youth was not much to worry about physically but Carl would not fight him. That didn't stop the kid.

He got Carl down to the ground and began pounding Carl's face to pieces. Not that Carl seemed to mind. He carried on a calm conversation with me the entire time this kid was beating on his face. I was yelling at him to fight back.

"I can't Ken! If I hit him I'll get double jeopardy!"

In the service, you can be charged and sentenced with a crime in civilian land and then charged and sentenced for the very same crime once on base. Their rationale is that you were not allowed to be in trouble in the first place so you get in trouble for getting in trouble. Double punishment. Probably more to it than that legally but that's what it amounted to in reality.

"I believe he has hit you enough to justify self-defense Carl! Hit him the fuck back!"

But he wouldn't. He was also a bit of a pacifist. I had no such moral qualms. I couldn't take it anymore. I walked over to the kid who was sitting on Carl's chest and got a handful of his long hair. I yanked him upward while simultaneously jumping up myself, bringing his body even higher. Then I drove his head down into the pavement with all my bodyweight on top. When I rolled him over he was no longer recognizable. Face was just destroyed.

I didn't get long to celebrate my victory though. Now the rest of the mob wanted my ass. I reacted fast. I got the kid in a chokehold that crushes the windpipe. Boot Camp 101. I rolled onto the ground and rolled his body on top of mine. Then I clarified the situation for the youngsters.

"There are more of you than I can take. We all know that. But I'll tell you this: If any of you take another step towards me your friend is dead. I'll crush his fucking throat. If I'm gonna lose then I'm taking him with me. Your choice."

Of course they had to test me and they all moved a little closer. So I gave his neck a squeeze and he gurgled and jerked around a bit. He sounded bad.

"I mean it! I'll take him out. I don't give a fuck!"

So they backed down and then the cops arrived.

Everything was a lot calmer then. The cops chilled everybody out. Then the father of the kid whose car I had hit showed up. We got to talking and I stayed extremely polite. He was irate and yelling about how sick he was of drunken Marines terrorizing his town. He couldn't be calmed. I stayed cool as long as I could but ultimately realized he was just becoming more and more amped. So then I lost it. I slammed him up against a car and berated his manhood. I argued how I'd already done right by his son but now he'd pissed me off so I was gonna kick his ass. So on and so forth.

A cop pulled me off of him. He got me cooled down and then told me to keep an eye on my friend. Now it gets funny. Carl is finally pissed off enough to fight. He wants to fight right now. I put him in his truck and closed the door. I promised the cop that I would keep him calm. I no longer said those words when a blur of activity flashed past me. It was Carl.

He ran past all of us too fast for anyone to stop him. He ran right for the car of the guy who'd beat him. The guy was sitting in the front seat. He jumped high in the air, letting out his trademark squeal (his voice cracked when he got excited). He threw a punch straight through the windshield and hit the guy in the face inside where he sat. Incredible! I'd never seen anything like that!

Somehow—we got out of all that with no charges being pressed! Some Jugs who'd been nearby took us back to base. They had seen the whole thing and were just about to jump in to help us but the cops showed up too fast. You gotta pick your battles so they held back.

We stopped at a store on the way back to base and bought a sixpack and a quart of beer for the room. We had a couch in our room and I went straight for it once we were in. I was out cold. I was awakened by someone who was not a close friend. I couldn't figure out what he was doing in my room. Then I noticed many guys in my room. They were using brooms to sweep water out into the hall and out the back door.

There was about two inches of water across our entire floor. I hadn't been back from Japan for long and in my state of mind I figured that's where I was and a typhoon must have hit. I looked at the windows but they were fine. I was flummoxed! I asked what the hell was going on.

"Ask your drunk roommate. This is all his fault."

Carl had jumped into the shower to wash off all his blood. He'd passed out and his naked ass covered the drain in the floor. He flooded the room. The only reason anyone knew this was because the guy who lived below us had complained of the rain falling on his stereo equipment. We were now officially in some deep shit. Of course, it got worse.

The next day we learned first-hand who everyone in our chain of command was. Met 'em all face to face. On top of each desk we stood before was the offending quart and sixpack of beer. We were not allowed to have beer in the barracks stateside. We were up on a lot of charges.

When we got to the Colonel we learned there was more hell to pay. He'd just received a call from the mother of the kid whose face I'd mashed and whose windshield was destroyed. Talked to her personally. She mentioned, among other things, a distinct fear of Marines she'd newly acquired.

The Colonel was how should I say it? Less than pleased with our actions. We were ordered to pay for her windshield and we had to each write a letter of apology to the lady. I doubt those letters soothed her frazzled nerves much but we did our best. Hard to be humble when you're busy being infuriated but we managed. We had to pay for the first car I'd hit as well.

In the midst of all this, it was decided that I had a drinking problem. Who knew?

I went to Level One. Again. In a sense I lucked out there. I should've been sent to detox and the year of suffering that went with it or kicked out on a General Discharge. That's what I needed but I wasn't even close to thinking I even HAD a problem let alone stop drinking. So I went to treatment reluctantly. Their rationale with repeating me was that the prior program had not been of sufficient quality to teach me the error of my ways. Each base ran their own gig in this fashion. So, with a heavy heart I began a new round.

Ken's note: Nights like these cause PTSD. Post Traumatic Stress Disorder is an anxiety disorder that can develop after experiencing one or more terrifying events in which grave physical harm occurred or was threatened. It is a severe and continuous emotional reaction to an extreme psychological trauma. This can be kicked off by many things: someone's actual death or a threat to your life or someone else's life, serious physical injury, or a threat to your safety so severe that you just can't cope with it. Profound psychological and emotional trauma, apart from any actual physical harm will plant a nice case of it in you, too. Often times, however, the two are combined.

This is the same PTSD a war vet feels. You cannot absorb this much violence, cannot hurt people like this, cannot deal with the massive punitive stresses it causes, cannot hold that all in, as I did for years, and not have it one day come back out.

It came out of me as psychotic rage when I drank and did so every single time I drank when I was bipolar. I was a threat to society and myself. Totally.

You may have PTSD, too. A life like this IS a war!

REST IN PEACE MARINE

The only friend who ever died on me did so during my first hitch in El Toro. I was one of the last people to see him alive. We were at Blacky's room. Blacky was Irish, like straight off the boat. I never understood how he was able to get in but I could care less. He was some piece of work. He owned a lot of books, was a genius, enjoyed motorcycling, drinking, and slugging Robe. He was one of the living legends. Only wore black, hence...

Mike was there too. Everyone was Robing but I couldn't tolerate drinking any that night. It was just too damn disgusting. So we had gone earlier to the pharmaceutical section of a nearby supermarket to find a substitute. I looked for the dextro (the cough suppressant) in all the products on the shelf. I found it in the same dosage in Comtrex Multi Cold Symptom capsules. Great! Now I can Robe without having to deal with the taste. I made a grave error in not taking into consideration the other ingredients for the rest of the cold symptoms.

At the room, Mike took two from me because he actually had a cold and I ate the rest of the box. I don't remember the rest of the night. I know I was Robing for a few hours but something went real wrong shortly thereafter. I was in some kind of Purgatory that was causing me to lose hold of my soul.

The following lasted for three entire days: I couldn't sleep but I was exhausted. I was light sensitive. My pupils would not stay one size. I could not comprehend what my senses were telling me. I was starving but nothing tasted good. I couldn't focus on anything. I'd begin walking someplace and after a few steps not have any idea where it was that I had to go. I was hot. I was cold. The two never evened out. I barely knew what was real. My friends had to babysit me this whole time.

Somewhere in all this I get the news that Mike had died. Drowned in some lake nearby under peculiar circumstances. I was devastated. I caved in the side of an a/c with one punch. I hit it so hard I don't know how my hand didn't break.

I had just begun to know him. He was amazingly fun to be around. He also was a bit of a living legend. I truly felt lucky that this guy was in my life and had been looking forward to the adventures we'd undertake. I'd partied with him before so I knew what I'd just lost. His dying hurt me so bad. I wasn't the only one who felt this way. Over 200 people showed up for his funeral. That kind of messed me up for a little while.

NO REALLY. I'M INNOCENT!

I again managed to get thrown in jail somewhere around this time. Some guy was pushing my buttons in a bar. I tried to ignore him but he wasn't having it. I was punching him in the face with my right hand as they were cuffing my left. I thought my ass was toast but the cops spoke to everyone at the bar and they vouched that the guy wasn't leaving me any choice.

But due to the brutality I displayed, they felt it best that I cool off for the night in the can. No charges. They were even laughing. That one never made it back to command. However, I felt the need for a change of venue so when I got word a detachment was being formed for Iwakuni, I requested a spot and was accepted.

Ken's note: A change in locale rarely changes life for the better. That's AA 101. The problem is you. You move and the problem magically comes with you. Granted, if you leave the hood for the burbs, that's one thing. But you know what thing I mean.

KEN JENSEN

CAN'T WE ALL JUST GET ALONG?

It felt good to be back in Japan. Because of a fluke I was running the whole shop as a Corporal for three weeks. Then we got a new boss. He was strict and he had just as much of an edge in him as I did. We clashed. I'd say attitude-wise we were neck and neck. So rank won the fight.

It sucked working for this guy. I had maybe three bosses I couldn't tolerate out of the maybe fifteen I'd worked for and even then I got two of the bad ones to come around to my way of thinking. Not this one guy. We nearly came to blows. I'm pretty sure we both wanted to kick each other's ass. But he left relatively soon and one of the best bosses I've ever had took his place.

My new Gunny was hard core Marine. Lifer. He and his men were polar opposites but he was convinced that we knew our job well. He instantly sized us up and got it right.

"Here's how it's gonna be. You guys know what you're doing and you're good at it. I know you do not like the formalities of being a Marine so to speak but you work hard. I also know that if you're working unsupervised that it doesn't matter because you are doing the right things. Therefore, whenever someone with higher rank starts giving you shit, you will NOT argue with them. Just be respectful, keep doing what you know needs to be done and send that person to see me. I will then tear them a new asshole for fucking with my men because I know you are in the right. That way the job gets done and you animals stay out of trouble.

You just stay out there making me look good and I will sit my fat ass in the main office with the rest of the bosses drinking our coffee, and I will leave you alone. I will defend you guys with everything at my disposal. Deal?"

He was the best boss I ever worked for and I respected him with all my heart.

Ken's note: Insanity and shame. I left Iwakuni without saying goodbye to that man, the one I respected more than all the rest. It was because of some things I did while drunk, including a guy I beat up and didn't remember, and the Gunny could've turned me in to the drug and alcohol people, but didn't.

But he did have a heart to heart with me that was more than I could tolerate at the time. I was filled with shame and confused by the psychotic break you'll read about next.

So I left without saying goodbye and felt like a shit for decades after. He showed me my true self and I found it to be more honesty than I could handle. Oh my God, how that short period hurt me.

THE LUNATIC IS IN MY HEAD

It was around this time that my evil ways were causing me to suffer. I got busted for public drunkenness again and I think a touch of assault was thrown in. I was pounding on some guy just because it was his lucky night to cross my path and I needed a target.

Cops showed up. They hurt me pretty good. One humungous MP and an NIS guy (sort of the FBI of the Navy). Not sure how NIS became involved but that night I wasn't sure of anything except the fact that I was extremely pissed...at everything.

I was in the back of a patrol car trying to kick out the windows. I distinctly remember telling the female MP that "she didn't have a hair on her ass!" if she didn't fight me like a man.

Big Boy took me out, had me cuffed behind my back, lifted me up like a sack of potatoes (I weighed about 225 at the time—this was a big dude), held me horizontally over the little fence in front of the barracks—and let go.

The fence posts were metal, about one inch square and maybe four inches apart. He dropped me right on my ribs. Nothing broke. I don't know how. But he achieved his goal of calming me down. I just hung there wrapped in pain. Felt like I just got hit by a truck. I was seeing stars. I never knew you could see stars without getting hit in the head.

He patted me on the back and said, "Yeah, you just rest a bit."

Shit, he wasn't even in a bad mood. I behaved for a little while longer. I'm not sure why I wasn't taken to a cell but I was being led to my room. The rage kicked in again. Blinding rage. I wanted to kill something—anything. That's when the NIS guy permanently altered my physiology.

It was clear that I was not going to calm down. So, hands still cuffed behind my back, this man lifted my hands up behind my head. This forced me to my knees in pain. He kept lifting, which caused me to go face down on the concrete and kept going until both my shoulders dislocated and my hands went flush with the floor somewhere over my head.

Sounded like two grenades going off in my ears when the shoulders went. The pain was exquisite. I almost passed out. Sure made me forget all about those bruised ribs. He waited a minute then asked if I was gonna be good. Truthfully, that last move really kicked the snot out of me. I told him I was good and he let me up. He brought my arms back around and they both popped back in.

I was left in my room with my roommate and the Duty Sgt. who I had tried to beat the crap out of earlier. As soon as we were alone, I attacked the Sgt. again. Got ahold of his neck, lifted him up about a foot off the ground and pulled back to smash his head.

"Fuckin' MP!" I remembered yelling. My roommate stopped me.

"Ken! He's not a cop! Put him down!"

I finally ran out of steam and passed out.

I was in a spot of trouble over all that. Now I was in Level Two. Good people actually. I liked the counselors but I wasn't really in a receptive mood.

My mind started to slip. I was in a black, black place. In my head I had visions of dark storms. I was losing it and I knew it but I didn't know what to do about it.

I became fascinated with cutting myself for a while. It had something to do with being able to take the pain. Something about seeing myself bleed somehow placated me too.

I became more masochistic. I say more because my life was already the paragon of masochism. I just upped the ante. I felt like I had to suffer physically due to how I felt mentally. I can't explain it. It just was.

I think it gave me a sense of control by managing my pain. I cut myself where people could see so I think it made me feel tough too. I was feeling weak mentally so I had to prove my strength physically.

None of this was conscious. I'm not quite sure who was running the show then but it wasn't me. Even now as I write this, I can't believe it was me. I hope this at least partly convinces you that if you're in a bad way you can still pull out. You can get better. I did.

Ken's note: Seriously kids, you don't want to attain this level of crazy. If anything about you is like this old me you've been reading about, then please be sure to enact my system in your life.

IT'S JUST A FLESH WOUND

I switched it up one night at Terry's Place, my favorite bar in the whole damn world. I put out cigarettes on my chest and abdomen, laughing like the maniac I was the whole time. Just couldn't seem to hurt myself enough. Still have the scars.

It wasn't all inward, this destruction. I could share with the crowd too. A young guy new to our shop was fucking with me one day while I cut myself with a razor blade.

He was mimicking awe as he said, "Wow, man. That's cool. You're a real tough guy. Can you cut me too so I can be tough like you?"

My Navajo friend tried to save this guy from me because he just wasn't gettin' it. I believe he was too young to have ever dealt with a truly unbalanced mind like mine and too stupid to stop.

I said, "Sure. I'll cut you. But know this: after I do it nothing better come back my way or I will beat you into a coma. I mean it, I'll hurt you."

He said, "Cool. Do it," and put his hand down on the desk. It went down so fast I don't think he realized what had just happened to him.

I cut him fast and deep. Laid open most of the meaty part of his hand next to his thumb. For a moment it was just a thin red line then the wound popped open and I could see down into his hand. As soon as the blood began to flow he started to freak out. I grabbed him and pulled him face to face.

"Better invent a story and go get that stitched up. My name comes up, I'll lie and deny and then I'll beat the shit out of you first chance I get."

Then I pushed him away. He looked around for help but Chief just stared at him with that stoic Indian face and said, "See ya stupid shit? I told you to leave him alone. He's for real. He's fucked up. But you wouldn't listen. If Kenny gets busted, I'LL kick your ass for him!"

Chief. One of my best friends to this day.

Ken's note: Cutting and other forms of self-mutilation is very common amongst bipolar people. It is a severely critical cry for help. I didn't even know until maybe 15 years later, that how I was cutting myself, was a commonality. If you cut to relieve the pressure and pain within, know that I can help you stop. And know that you need to stop if it's only at the oddity stage for you like it was for me then.

KEN JENSEN

THANK GOODNESS THERE ARE PROFESSIONALS TO HELP US

At group they noticed the hand wounds on me. The lady counselor considered them a cry for help. I didn't think so at the time but I suppose they were. I got sent to a psychiatrist. By now I knew I was in a bad way. I decided to open up and see if someone could help me feel better.

The doctor, an officer, entered the room. He was much older, high ranking and his chest was covered in ribbons. John—fucking—Wayne. I made the immediate mistake of calling him "Doc" and it was all downhill from there.

Instead of helping me, he reprimanded me for not calling him "sir." I tried to ignore his militaryness and proceeded to tell him how I felt and gave him some background. I knew for a fact that I was losing my mind and his official summary was that I drank too much, was in fine physical shape, and seemed a little immature.

Yeah, well, I was those things but he seemed to ignore the whole Stephen King-like scenario that was my mental playing field. I was in an alternate reality that was based on pain; nothing but the most evil of thoughts, and he's telling me to grow up. I removed the report from my record figuring it could damage me in some way down the road. I'll never know if that was the way to go or not.

Ken's note: Oh, how I could carry on about the woeful state of the Mental Health Care system. It would take up too much space, so just know that if you've tried their way and found it to be less than satisfactory in results, at least have the logical open mindedness to give my way a try.

C'mon. If you're a veteran of that system, then what are you trying to prove by continuing on with them? Definition of insanity: Doing the same thing, over and over, and expecting different results. Think about that.

KEN JENSEN

MUST'VE HAD A SALE ON CRAZY AT THE PX

Then came the night my roommate flipped out. This was simply spectacular. He wanted out. Just fed up with military life. He totally orchestrated what came next. He got crazy drunk one night during Black History month. There were big banners hanging from the overhead steam pipes above the street and mentions of the occasion everywhere you went. Hoagie was the furthest thing from racist but it was a convenient operating platform to stage a mental breakdown over.

I was in my room with Chief. We were Robing and we'd done way too much. We were clinging to a fine thread praying to God the ride would end but that wouldn't be for many long hours later. We were out of our minds. At one point we were cheek to cheek looking at our faces in the mirror.

Chief asked, "Can you see my eyes? I can't. I see yours but not mine."

Then he yelled out, "Ken!"

I faced him and asked, "What?"

He said, "I don't know...ya know?" and cracked up. We had some profoundly disturbing moments that night.

We heard the far away voice screaming in the night.

"That sounds like Hoagie."

I opened the door and saw my roommate heading straight up the center of the empty street. He was screaming racial slurs at the top of his lungs. Just *the* most vicious shit! Even in my frame of mind I knew he was lost, out of control. Chief and I tried to mentally prepare ourselves for when Hotel (the other nickname for Hoagie) would reach the room. It was pointless. We were too far gone.

Hotel came in the room and was crazed! He'd reached that stage of drunkenness in which he should have passed out from liver failure but the animal in him wouldn't quit. He started destroying the room.

Then he pulled his Katana, a Japanese long sword, out of his wall locker and began slashing wildly at everything. Now it was becoming dangerous. I tackled him and tried to subdue him but I was too poisoned from Robe. I had no strength. Normally I could kick his ass without even trying. I was holding on but he was bashing my head into the wall so I let go. I couldn't control him. Keep in mind that right at this point I was not even sure what was real. I was in an extremely altered state of mind. The hardest Robe ever.

He got up and started yelling racist shit again at the top of his lungs. We got a knock at the door. It was two black guys who lived close by. They were pissed. It was psychotic because we were all friends, Hotel included. I explained to them that this wasn't normal and I was trying to get him under control. They said they understood but that if I didn't quiet him down soon they would call the MPs. Now I was getting worried for Hotel. I had no clue why this was happening but the first rule was to always cover your man's back. I had to get help.

I headed down the hall where some guys lived who I partied with a lot. I knocked. The door opened and instantly I knew I was fucked.

My friend Kenny is talking to me but he's not facing me and he's not making sense. Stu is crawling around on all fours and seems disturbed by the interruption. He looks confused and about to cry. Ray is in the background wearing his bunny slippers doing "Ray-robics," a high stepping type of exercise he only did when he was whacked. All three were totally twisted on Robe. They were way beyond where even Chief and I were. No good.

I headed back to the room and saw that the MPs were already there. Hotel was arrested. There was more crap he pulled as this took place, including him begging the MPs to, "Hit me with the sticks! Hit me with the sticks you bitches!" and some really funny other shit. They ended up violently taking him to the floor. And he loved it!

I went out to the squad car to get any info I needed to tell my boss on Monday. I was desperately trying to hide the fact that I was currently an extra in a Pink Floyd/Grateful Dead video but I pulled it off.

The following day he was brought before whomever and told he must enter Level Two. This was his second major alcohol offense. He refused. He was threatened that this was automatic grounds for discharge and he said, "Yeah, I know." We rotated back to the States and a couple months later he was discharged with a less than honorable but he was happy as a clam. Mission accomplished. He never meant a single thing he said that night. But he knew timing when he saw it.

Ken's note: Again, I share this story to show you how much violent, drug soaked lunacy has been tucked away into my subconscious. You simply cannot eternally absorb moments like these and not pay for it down the road. Helllooo bipolar!

WE GOT THE WHISKEY AND WE GOT THE TIME. NOW IF THERE WAS JUST SOMETHING TO DO

I returned to El Toro. The adventure never stopped. I just became darker about it all. Here's a standout moment: It's 11 am on a Saturday and I am in a mall with one of my best friends and coworker, Matt. We are very drunk. We have large Burger King cups that are half-full of soda and half whiskey. We've been drinking since dawn.

I notice there are kids everywhere, maybe four or five years old. Lots of 'em. I talk low to Matt without facing him. I don't want to project anything to the crowd.

"I'm about to do something fucked up. Do NOT react."

He says, "Go."

A happy little tot comes charging my way. Right as he gets near me I extend my open hand and catch his forehead like a basketball. In one smooth motion I change his trajectory and send him face first into a store window. Just hard enough for the reaction I wanted. I didn't want to actually hurt the kid. Just upset him.

He hits the floor bawling, crying his eyes out but seems unable to clearly convey to his worried mother what just happened. Nobody knew. Matt and I never even changed pace.

Matt says, "That was fucked up. Let me do the next one."

I chuckle and whisper, "Help yourself. Plenty to pick from."

A little girl with ponytails bouncing behind her comes running past. Matt casually sticks out his foot and sends her spinning like a star across the highly polished floor. She's crying up a storm, concerned mom, same deal but again, no one knows it's us! We continued to lay out about a dozen kids this way. We reached the end of the hall. We looked back only then on our handiwork.

"Incredible. There's bodies everywhere."

"Yeah. Someone's gonna do the math. Shall we?"

"Let's." And we headed out the exit. Once outside we ran like crazy for the car laughing hysterically the whole way.

"I can't believe we just did that!"

"That is without a doubt one of the most fucked up things we have ever done! Awesome!"

I lost track of how many times I said that while enlisted.

Ken's note: If this isn't a sign of warped mentality, nothing is. I completely lost the urge to care for other's feelings while I was in. Later in life, this transforming of "people" into "targets" or "victims," became even more pronounced within me.

HEAVY METAL MUSIC DOES NOT CAUSE VIOLENCE—BUT IT SURE HELPS WITH THE FLOW

I was fortunate enough to be in California during the height of the Heavy Metal era. Late eighties, early nineties. I saw all the big bands: Ozzy, Metallica, AC/DC, Megadeth, Anthrax, Judas Priest, and a handful of Grateful Dead shows, just to keep well rounded, to name some. Every concert has a story attached to it. A few are epic.

I was a severe metal head. Every show had audiences numbering in the tens of thousands. I was blessed to have been able to experience my music at its finest moment in its area of mightiest fan support. I was aware of this situation. I knew I was living history.

It was at a Metallica show that I tried tripping on acid in public for the first time. Talk about crowd energy! Violence was in the air. Fantastic night! Not so fantastic for the guy who decided to try my patience.

I was nearing my peak. I had a tenuous hold on reality but I was doing ok. So long as nothing dramatic took place I would probably stay that way. I was on the very razor's edge of sensory overload. That's when somebody bodychecked me from behind. The effect inside my mind was staggering. But I recovered and let it ride. Didn't even turn to see who had slammed into me. Fuck it. It's Metallica after all. Shit will happen. I calmed back down.

Maybe a minute passed before I got bodychecked again. That's it. Can't take it no more. I turned to address my new friend. He was a skinny kid with a ton of hair and no shoes. Looked like Jesus Christ.

He explained to me that he wanted to get to the front row. We were way up in nosebleed at an amphitheater. I tried to get him to calm down. My mood was good. I explained how there was an apparent football team hired for security. These guys were literally smashing in the heads of any who rushed the stage with Maglite flashlights. I was watching them lay out kids unconscious, all night. Told my new buddy that he didn't need that shit and there was plenty of room to hang out with us. He was obviously tweaked on something, as were we. Let's enjoy the trip together. He lost it.

"FUCK YOU! I gotta get to the FRONT FUCKING ROW!" and began to try and push past me.

That's when I ruined his evening. Probably ruined his entire next week.

I said, "Here, lemme give you a hand."

With that I reached back with my left hand and wrapped up a bunch of his hair. I reached back with my right and got ahold of the front of his shirt. In one smooth move I hoisted him up onto my right shoulder then simply shot-putted him six rows down into what appeared to be a pile of bikers. He knocked down about ten guys on impact.

I'll give him credit. He was up on his feet in a flash. He looked up at me and growled. Hands bunched up into fists. He wanted to fight! Keeping in mind that I was peaking on acid, I now wanted his blood running free through my fingers.

I hollered down to him, "C'mon!" and motioned him towards me with my hands.

He never stood a chance. Took one step before the bikers dragged him down into their midst. They thrashed him. Couldn't even see him. Just fists and flying feet. I saw lights bobbing up towards the fracas. Security was coming. BIG, BIG dudes.

The kid's body suddenly flew up into the air on an arc that landed him on the concrete steps. Security talked briefly with the bikers then they just dragged the kid's lifeless form down the stairs, his head bouncing freely on each step. It was phenomenal! Ernie, another best friend/coworker and fellow metal head, leaned over to me and yelled, "I was just about to do the same thing to him but as I turned to do it his feet were already flying past my face! Good job Ken! Fuck that fucker!"

As we were leaving the concert area to go back to Ernie's monster truck we encountered a young metal head sitting on a fence. He was wounded. Looked as if he might have been one of the kids charging the stage.

His skull was cracked wide open. Blood covered most of his head and torso. Yet he seemed nonplussed. Just sat there bobbing his head to a tune only he could hear. I stopped our little group to inspect.

"Check this out. You can see right down to his brain! No shit! Look!"

We all took turns looking into this kid's split skull. He didn't seem to know we were there. We figured he was probably near death. It truly was a bad head wound. His skull was cracked about an inch wide and all the way through. We offered to take him to a hospital.

"Nah. I'm good." He smiled and was very pleasant.

"OK then. How about we get an ambulance for you?"

"Nope. I'm good!"

So we left him. Hell, we tried. We all agreed on the walk back to the truck that we had been talking to a dead man.

Much more happened this night. We were just getting warmed up. But all I really wanted to do here was to give you a little more insight to my mad history and acknowledge how cool it was to have been a metal head at this point in time. It was an integral part of my personality. I'm calm now, really, but I still love metal.

AND YOU THINK YOU GOT PROBLEMS

I hadn't been back from Japan too long when I was approached by a committee consisting of the Barracks Sgt. and some others. I thought I was in trouble but this was not a normal scenario whatsoever.

Turns out I was in trouble but not the way I thought. For some reason somebody had to room with Willy. Because I was one of his closest friends I was a clear choice. I was also told I was the only one who was as crazy as he was and that we'd be a good match.

"Fuck—that!" I said. "The fact that I do know Willy well is enough to let me know I don't want to live with him. I ain't doin' it!"

They begged me. "You're the only one who stands a chance man! He'll kill anyone else we put with him. You know how to control him!"

They were right so I obliged. Willy was a good friend, he really was. But he was also a caveman. He could become incredibly mean, Satan-mean, he was phenomenally strong, and he drank too much. I once watched him drink an entire half keg of beer by himself in one 12-hour period.

When he was drunk I had to be very careful and keep my guard up. I loved drinking with him. I got off on his homicidal energy. When it came to drinking and being unpredictably psychotic we were pretty evenly matched. The problem was that once he was good and hammered, anyone he saw was a potential victim, including me.

Some nights we'd drink together for hours having lots of laughs. We fed off of each other's personas. We were a violent pair. That was our underlying drive when we drank. Evil, dark juju. But Will had a switch. It would go off unexpectedly.

We'd be laughing and carrying on, everything just fine. I'd get up to make a fresh cocktail and the room would suddenly get awfully quiet. I could feel it. The change. When I'd turn around, he'd be glaring at me. It was a severely menacing look, full of hate.

When that happened I'd make a mondo-sized drink and leave the room with it. Wouldn't even say goodbye. I knew Will was only seconds away from kicking my ass and that it would probably hurt. I could brawl and wrestle but Willy was also a kick boxer. Forgot to mention that earlier. Adds an extra dimension to the overall picture doesn't it? I also don't believe he was capable of feeling pain. I'd come back when I figured he'd cooled down.

Ken's note: OK. Please bear with the Willy stories. This one man alone caused me to face an aspect of survival few will ever be forced to see. I lived with, caused, and survived more violence and hatred with him, than at any other time in my life. And I liked it! My time with Willy changed something in me that needs to be made clear. It affected me for decades after. It was a lot to overcome.

WILLY PART TWO: NEVER MIX BOOZE, UNIDENTIFIED SUBSTANCES AND GRAVITY

We had a rare 96-hour weekend. Four days off. Will and I decided to go on a drinking binge. All four days no matter what. It may surprise you to know that I'd never drank more than two nights in a row, at least not heavily. I couldn't take the pain of too many successive hangovers. And believe it or not I often went running and I always lifted weights. But this time I decided to go for it.

I only drank for three days. It was just too much. But in those three days we drank 6 cases of beer, 4 fifths of whiskey, a handful of pints of various liquors, and even managed to fit in some visits to some bars in town. I almost died from that weekend but only partly because of drinking.

On the third night we were running out of steam. Decided we needed a chemical pick me up. I only knew of one guy who might be able to help us and I didn't know him well. I knew he could get crystal meth so I approached him. He sold me some white powder that was supposed to be crystal. Me and Will snorted it and climbed up through the hatch onto the roof of the barracks. Something different to do.

Not long after, reality took a vacation. I thought I was a medieval king and the bean fields around the base were the feudal lands. I was gone. Who knows what the hell Willy was thinking? We sat face-to-face, Indian style, and decided to trade punches for a while. We both got pretty banged up from that.

We soon tired of that and Will got up and took a walk to the edge of the roof. He dropped over the edge and swung side to side by his fingertips. I walked over to inspect the situation. He just looked at me as I stomped on his fingers 'til he fell. Neither of us had said a word. He fell flat on his back onto the third floor catwalk. Concrete. He hit hard and didn't move. Never made a sound. I don't even know why I did it. I wasn't mad. Shit. I didn't feel anything.

My work done I returned to the center of the roof and sat down. A little while later Will showed up. Nothing was said about anything by either one of us. It was like nothing had happened.

Maybe an hour goes by and I decide to return to the room. Willy follows me to the hatch.

Then he grabs me and says, "Here, let me give you a hand."

He effortlessly lifted me above the two feet of raised wall around the hatch then threw me through the hole. I fell about 10 or 12 feet and landed on my shoulder, neck and side of my head. Somehow, nothing broke and I didn't get knocked out. But I was in pain. A lot of it. I knew he'd just hurt me bad.

He climbed down the ladder and scooped me up then threw me down the first flight of stairs. Did the same on the second flight. On the second deck he put me over his shoulder and used my head as a battering ram to open the swinging steel doors. Again for the next set. Then again at our room.

He tossed me on the floor in the middle of the room like a used rag. Guess he was a little ticked about the whole finger stomping thing. I blacked out. I woke up 12 hours later. I could barely walk. Every movement was agony. There wasn't a spot on me that didn't hurt. I asked Will what the hell happened last night.

"I don't know but we hurt each other pretty bad. I ain't never hurt this bad. And I was thinking some pretty strange shit. I don't think we should ever do anything like that ever again."

"Agreed."

I went to bed and slept another 12 hours then got up for work. That day I talked to a Sgt. I could trust in such matters. He had been a biker before the Marines. Shotgun man for drug deals. If a deal went bad he started blasting everyone not in his club. That kind of thing.

I explained how I was feeling and thinking on the roof. Told him I wasn't sure what happened but that it was new.

"You were on PCP man. I wouldn't buy any more shit from that guy of yours if I were you."

I took his advice to heart.

Ken's note: I did a lot of drugs while in. This was just the warm up. But, I think the unexpected PCP may have done some lasting harm. Just a hunch.

WILLY PART THREE: JUST A TYPICAL FRIDAY AFTERNOON

I'm having a pleasant Friday afternoon with Brad. We're tripping our faces off on some really good acid. We're watching this fantastic cult movie called "Psychout." Jack Nicholson is about 19 in this flick and Bruce Dern thinks he's Jesus. All about the counter-culture in the '60s. The movie's so bad it's beautiful. Especially from our perspective this day.

Brad and I are having a blast sharing complimentary hallucinations. I'm seeing things on the screen that aren't there and he's confirming that he sees the same things and narrates what they do next without me talking. But what I'm seeing matches what he's saying. Impossibly bizarre visions yet we both see them simultaneously. We're laughing nonstop. We really knew how to squeeze every possible ounce of fun out of situations like this.

Someone knocks on the door. Some guy is telling me I'm needed outside. I tell him I'm flying high on Vitamin A but he says it doesn't matter.

"Kenny, you gotta come quick. Willy just came home from leave. He's shitfaced and hollering for you! He's going crazy. You better come deal with him quick before he does something stupid!"

I'm entirely too wasted to deal with this. I'm not even on Earth. I ask Brad to come help me. Brad was a big boy, one of the few who could probably fight Will and live.

We find Willy out back behind the barracks. He goes berserk with happiness when he sees me. He's staggering drunk.

He yells, "Kenny!" and charges, laughing like a child as he draws near.

He jumps on my back, which completely destroys the version of reality I'd been currently working with. This was indeed too much for me to handle in my condition.

I ask Brad, "Where can we dump him? Who will take him? I can't do this, it's too much. I'm gonna freak out!"

"Let's try Couch's room."

So we cajole Willy into following us. We get to Couch's, which has an exterior hallway door, and knock on the steel door. Nothing. I put my ear up to the door but hear nothing at all.

"He must be out. Let's go somewhere else Will."

I jump over the low wall and join Brad on the grass.

Willy says, "Fuck that! You just didn't knock hard enough!"

With that he leans back and kicks the door open with one shot. Destroyed the latch and the deadbolt that had been locked in place. In that brief instant Brad and I see Couch with his two civilian buddies leaning over a contraption on the sink counter. They're freebasing cocaine. I had no idea this was one of his hobbies but I knew what I was seeing. Couch's heart rate had to be pretty high already. Can't imagine what it rocketed up to when that door blew in. He was beyond livid.

"What- the FUCK—are you doing?!" he screamed at Will.

"Fuck you. Gimme a beer." Willy hadn't even raised his voice. Just walked in and sat down.

That was enough. Couch hadn't seen me and Brad yet. We didn't want him to know we were responsible for bringing this shit down on him at this oh-so sensitive time. There wasn't anything Couch could do though. Willy could have easily massacred all three of them and Couch knew it. But still, we didn't want him to know our part. We ran. We laughed like lunatics the whole way. Given our lifestyle we could appreciate the fear Couch probably just lived through but that didn't make it any less funny to us! Plus, shit, we were trippin'!

We made it back to the end of our barracks. We took a moment to reflect, me leaning on Brad's shoulder. That's when we noticed the cracks in the concrete wall. My! Weren't they just crawling and moving about the place?!

We got fairly engrossed with watching the snake-like motion of the cracks when the second deck door flew open. It was Rob. He's drunk and he has also just returned from leave. He's completely amped up and just starts jabbering.

"Hey fuckers! Guess what? I have to go check in from leave at headquarters and give a urine sample."

This was a new rule they imposed on us so you couldn't enjoy your damn vacation. That's how we looked at it anyway.

"There ain't no fucking way I'm gonna pass it! I think all the weed will turn it the wrong color!"

He keeps talking as he comes down to us. He gets near and suddenly stops talking. He's looking close at our stupid, grinning faces.

He says real soft, "You fucks. You got any more?"

We couldn't hold it in any longer. We busted up laughing and told him no. We were out. Now he's mad at us. Lord, the bad things he called us! He jumps in his jeep and drives, while massively intoxicated, to headquarters so he could give them his dirty urine.

As we knew he would be, he got brought up on charges for drugs in his system. But I'm telling you, nobody DIDN'T care like this guy. He was Mister Cool. At his office hours he actually put together a case to argue his innocence and won! Only guy I ever knew who got caught red-handed but escaped conviction. He's a lawyer now, I kid you not.

Ken's note: People always seem to think that the military world is drug free due to our training. I never even knew about drugs UNTIL I joined! We were kids like all other kids. If anything, we were more adventurous and risk taking. Drugs were just one more adventure. And California was Drug Heaven. Coke and weed, specifically, had a way of just appearing out of thin air at parties, it seemed.

NICOTINE CAN BE A GATEWAY DRUG

I had one of them blue ribbon hangovers. The kind that would make Clint Eastwood weep. It was a very hot summer day. That made it much worse. I walked over to Kenny's room, the guy who was of no help to me in the Hotel/Iwakuni incident. I was simply visiting and moving around as it hurt too much to hold still.

"You look like shit."

I explained exactly which outer ring of Hell I was currently in.

"You want that hangover to go away?"

Of course I did. I knew what he was getting at too but I sensed something new was coming my way. I didn't care. This pain had to go. Three of us crammed into the head in his room. They had a cigarette.

"Smoke this. We put some coke in the middle."

I'd never done that before but I really didn't care. I hurt so bad. I took two hits. The smoke felt like fiberglass in my throat. Too painful to inhale. I begged off anymore and walked back out into the room. I didn't feel anything. I figured I hadn't smoked enough. Then it hit me.

I had to sit down fast. The high that followed was exponentially better than anything I'd ever felt in my life. It just kept going up and up and up. Soon I was in the stratosphere. I could barely comprehend how good this felt. To this day it remains the best psychological sensation I've ever experienced. It only lasted ten minutes then it was gone. But so was my hangover.

The guys came out and offered me more.

"No thanks, man."

"Didn't you like it? You got off right?"

"That felt so fucking good that it's all I ever want to feel all day, every day. I now know why junkies steal from their parents and live in squalor. If I don't stop now, I'll never stop. I know myself too well."

I never did that again. One of the few times I employed rational thought.

KEN JENSEN

WILLY PART FOUR: THE DEATH OF KEN AND WILL

I fit in one more misadventure with Willy. He had just bought a nice car off of another Marine. It was fairly new and had a lot of power. To celebrate we went out to town together and really tied one on. Once we realized we couldn't keep going we decided to return to base. We actually employed some sensible foresight given the circumstances.

We both had a feeling that we might experience a bumpy ride on the way back. For the first time ever, we used our seatbelts. This move saved our lives. We also realized that we were too drunk to make it through the gate. The MPs would bust us for DWI as we tried to enter the base so we decided to head to Jimbo's house out in town, instead. We never made it.

We were on a very large civilian highway near the base perimeter. For some reason Willy began to accelerate and wouldn't back off. We were approaching 100 mph. I told Will to slow down. He told me he couldn't. I yelled at him, "What the fuck are you doing?!" He said he didn't know. I noticed he was white knuckling the wheel. Now I'm yelling at him to stop! He's not able. He's in some other reality that won't allow for that.

The last time I looked at the digital speedometer we were going 107 mph. Then Willy lost control. We came around a curve that wasn't really a curve at slower speeds. We slid across the left lane and went right into the base perimeter fence. We hit it lengthwise.

The car got all wrapped up in the chain link. We tore up 100 feet of fence. The car was rolling like a bullet. I don't know how many times we flipped. Inside the windows all blew up around us. Sounded like bombs each time another window exploded. We just went with it. We were actually having a blast! Screaming, hollering all sorts of shit at the top of our lungs. I remember yelling out, "This is fucking outstanding!"

The car collided with a couple of concrete posts protecting a 6-inch aboveground gas main. The poles did their job and that's one more reason why I'm still alive to tell any of this. Once the car stopped we did a quick self-check. We were fine! Just some scratches from the flying glass.

"Fuck this, Will! Get this pig moving before anyone spots us!"

The engine still turned over but it wouldn't start. Probably had something to do with the fact that it was actually now sitting between our legs. We realized it wasn't going to go so we crawled out the windows. That's when all the emergency vehicles showed up.

Once we got out it became clear how bad the wreck was. The car was destroyed. Looked like God had rolled it into a ball in his hands. One front wheel was bent sideways. The fence had ground down the louvers on the rear window.

The MPs, for once, actually helped us. They got in a big argument with the civilian police who were also present over whose jurisdiction we fell under. Because we were on base property it was decided that the MPs owned us and not the civilian cops. Legally speaking, that saved us jail sentences out in town. However, the MPs still seemed upset with us. Go figure.

One of them began verbally attacking Willy. He was stone-faced and silent. I could see the rage, with which I was so familiar, building up inside Will. I tried to intervene so Will wouldn't try to start brawling with the MPs. That's when I got officially busted. Up 'til that point there were no charges against me because I was a passenger. I was simply trying to explain to the MP that Will had to be handled just so. That's when the MP began arguing with me. I then of course flew off the handle instead of Will. I got charged with something. I was like—a professional asshole when I was drunk.

That's how I entered Level Two for the second time.

THE TWIN TERRORS GET THE HELP THEY NEED

My boss, another Gunny, was questioned as to my disposition. He was a worm of a guy. Never understood how he got into the Marines. None of us respected him. But he informed the authorities that I had a real violent streak in me. That sealed my fate treatment-wise. When I asked him why the fuck he would say something like that he answered, "Well, you ARE!"

Well sure I was. But that wasn't the point. I felt he had betrayed me. But it was out of my hands by then.

The ironic thing here is that I actually learned something this time around. Not that I used any of it to my advantage at that time. But I did get taught a bunch of things that meant a great deal to me later in life. I never forgot.

My circle of friends learned something from this as well. EVERYBODY drank and drove. Simple fact amongst most everyone that I knew. Our car wreck got everyone to thinking. The fact that we had veered across lanes really freaked everyone out. The dumb luck that we didn't hit head on with innocent people was heavily noted by many. We actually began to implement designated drivers. This was new to us. We also began wearing our seatbelts more often. I guess some good came out of it.

My first week in class I was totally unresponsive. I had no intention of participating. I was pissed—the fuck—off. I got handed an ultimatum at the end of that week. The Staff Sgt. in charge was going to roll me out of the class as a failed participant. That would then lead to me getting kicked out of the Marines under a less than honorable. Couldn't have that.

So I backpedaled and put on my humble face. Told him how I'd misinterpreted this and that. Quite a song and dance on my part. But it worked. I stayed in and from then on I participated. It was tough because I was so angry about being there.

I learned all about what goes on inside your mind and body when you consume alcohol and drugs. I realized that I really was going to have to quit drinking at some point. I just couldn't fathom doing it while still in. I continued drinking and drugging well after this period but what I learned played an integral part in deciding to quit drinking once I got out.

I should add that Willy finally got treatment himself. He was placed in Level Three. Bypassed the first two levels completely. And he did dry out and stayed dry for the rest of his time in the Marines. Even found a girlfriend at the hospital. I'm thinkin' God threw him a bone for finally taking care of himself.

WE'RE GOING TO WAR. WILL YOU BE WANTING ONE LUMP OF METH IN YOUR COFFEE OR TWO?

Saddam Hussein got his freak on and gears kicked into motion. It wasn't war yet, that was many months away but we knew it was coming. We tore up almost everything and packed it on a specially designed cargo ship to head for the Gulf.

At first many of us didn't want to go. Most guys my age were close to getting out. But once the idea settled in, we all got pumped and just wanted to go and waste a bunch of Iraqis. That was always hammered into us as our main mission. No matter what job we held, underneath we were all grunts. We were always told that if the shit hit the fan we dropped our wrenches and picked up our rifles. Honestly, none of us expected to do any fighting but we definitely wanted part in killing something.

We worked for three straight days and nights packing the ship. I had been on the base end tearing up equipment and sending it to the boat for a week. Now I was on the boat. The work was brutal. Everything had to be chained and cabled to the deck. Once it was all inside it had to be powered up. We worked our asses off. Guys were falling asleep where they stood. If they went completely unconscious, we stashed them out of the way and kept working.

A few of us were key players in getting things done in order. We had to stay awake. Somewhere around the third day I began hallucinating from fatigue. If two of us met and started a conversation it wouldn't be long before neither of us knew why we began talking in the first place. One of my friends approached me.

"Ken, you tired?"

"The fuck kind of stupid question is that? I can't even remember my own name."

"Come with me. You gotta meet this guy."

We went down five decks to the belly of the ship. This new guy from another unit was there waiting. He basically did the same thing me and my friend did work-wise.

He looked at my buddy and said, "Is he cool?"

"The coolest. Let's do it."

And that's how I finally got to try crystal meth. I gotta say I woke the hell up! Finished the final loading with a bang.

KEN JENSEN

THE PERFECT PARTY: DRINKING, WOMEN, AND A PSYCHOTIC BREAK

We left port only to return within the hour. Nothing worked right on the ship. Contractors had to come in from all over the country to get the ship up and running. In the meantime we were handed four days of liberty.

What a party. One night we drank all the tequila in the E-Club. I remember walking to this girl's house for some repeat fun and puking straight tequila, over and over. It was difficult to determine which of us was holding the other up. Word got out into town that 300+ Marines were on base with nothing to do and the women started pouring in. It was insane. We all got laid. It was impossible not to.

The married guys were using this shack on the pier. There was an endless stream of couples waiting their turn while the rest of us watched from the main deck. Every time a couple would come out there'd be a hundred of us waiting to yell out appropriate comments.

We lost one man to the party. Cupps never drank, ever. He wasn't right in the head when he was sober. We all knew it. Sort of had that UnaBomber thing going on. For some reason he pounded down a bunch of Jack Daniel's Iced Teas and headed back to the ship.

Couch, the Devil's right hand man, began tormenting Cupps, just because. That was Couch's primary job as he saw it. Stir up the shit. He was about one of the most evil dudes I knew the whole time I was in.

Cupps snapped and started chasing Couch all over the boat with his bayonet in hand. He's screaming at the top of his lungs that he's going to kill Couch and he meant it.

Couch got away and then Cupps vanished. After an extensive search Ernie found him sitting in one of the laundry rooms bleeding like a stuck pig. Remember that '70s movie with the little Voodoo doll? "Trilogy of Terror" I think it was called. Remember how Karen Black looked at the end once she was possessed? He looked just like that. He had carved the word "FUCK" into his forearm in big letters. That was it for Cupps. They didn't let him come play in the war. He got a psych discharge instead.

Ken's note: I had to show I wasn't the only one operating out in left field.

MY SHOP CAN KICK YOUR SHOP'S ASS

The ship broke down again before we'd even cleared the Aleutian Island chain off the tip of Alaska. We pulled into a Navy base in Adak. I saw permafrost for the first time. I was digging that. The ground only went down a few feet then became solid ice. You could see it where they cut through hills to make roads. It was so cold in the winter that the buildings were all connected by tunnels underground. Pretty trippy way to live.

We were handed three days of liberty here. It was total chaos. Crazier than the first port. The sailors at this base didn't mess around. Their bar was well stocked and they had a huge list of cocktail names they'd invented. We tipped the bartenders well and they poured heavily. We drank hard.

So much happened in these three days but the final night was classic. We already knew we were leaving the next day so everybody went at it extra hard that last night. Everyone stayed to the last minute. The bus back to the boat was packed. We got to the pier and I was at the very back. It was taking forever for the bus to empty. When I got to the front I saw why.

There was a female sailor driving. She was waiting with arms outstretched for every guy as he passed. She let all of us do whatever we wanted as we got to her. It would be too graphic to describe what I saw when I reached her but I took my turn as well. It was an awesome sendoff!

We walk onto the pier and my little buddy Todd has finally lost the ability to stay conscious. I throw him over my shoulder and walk us to the boat hundreds of yards away. By the time we reach the gangplank I am wiped out from drunkenness and physical exhaustion. Now I'm dead.

TJ my big TexMex buddy was already there, as was Matt. We are all 990 and we are the very last ones to board the boat. All four of us are completely shitfaced. I told T there was no way that Todd or I was going to make it up all those stairs. We needed a plan. TJ jumps right into it.

"OK. Lay Todd over my left shoulder. Matt can you walk? Good. You lean into me and hold Todd in place. Kenny, your legs are shot but can you crawl? Good. Get on my right side and I'll loop a finger through your pants and drag you as you crawl. Let's do this, fuckers!"

And that's how we made it back onto the ship. TJ was a tank. He provided all the power to get the four of us up those stairs. The whole way the rest of the 300 guys are cheering us on and yelling out all kinds of crap. TJ wouldn't quit.

This was gladiator life or death shit. He wouldn't fail us in front of an audience. We were 990 and had a reputation to uphold.

We reached the top and it took every bit of man in T to take that final step as we collapsed in a pile on the main deck. Just before he fell over TJ yelled, "990!" at the top of his lungs. The crowd went berserk. I swear to God it was one of the proudest moments in my life. It wasn't just the work involved. That whole display summed up perfectly the camaraderie and teamwork that existed in my shop. We had character.

Ken's note: To this very day, and I don't care what day that happens to be when you are reading this, these men are my brothers. I have a love for my friends that is separate and beyond any other bond I've ever had. When you know, and I mean, KNOW, you are surrounded by people who will freely die to protect you and they know you'll do the same…it's deep people. And I thank God forever, for bringing these guys into my life. My friends honor me. I honor them.

SHOULDA BOUGHT A FORD

The ocean voyage was mostly boring but had its moments. I saw flying fish, sea turtles, sea snakes, whales, dolphins, and many jellyfish. We were broke down again and moving along at all of 5 knots when I noticed "the bloom" as I called it.

There were jellyfish floating on the surface. They had big air sacs above the water about softball size. They had yards of tentacles and were about one foot apart from each other in all directions. They were everywhere. We floated through this bed of poison for hours. Had to be millions of them.

Storms almost sunk us a few times. We had a formation on the main deck. The Captain informed us that we had no power and were floating into the strongest category storm the sea could produce.

"We will die if we don't regain power. The storm is so fierce that we will not survive in the rafts either. We are on a collision course with this storm and I repeat we WILL NOT make it through. We WILL sink. We have a problem in the boilers and I don't have enough men to fix the problem in time. I just need volunteers to help."

Lotta hands went up. They got the boat fixed just as we met the storm. It turned north and we turned south so we just clipped the edge of it. Inside the ship it sounded like we were doomed anyway. The steel of the ship was being pounded and twisted by waves. The metal screamed and groaned. I didn't know it would be like that.

When you're below decks looking at all the steel that makes up the boat, it looks impervious. But in a storm you can hear the boat protesting. That night I made peace with everything. I figured we weren't going to see the morning. But we did.

KEN JENSEN

BREATHING, EATING AND ASSAULTS: THE FINER ASPECTS OF OCEAN TRAVEL

We got a safety lecture from the number two guy on the boat. It was about the firefighting system on board.

"The system is made with a gas that is heavier than oxygen. It puts out the fire by displacing the air it needs to burn. It's under extreme pressure. If the alarm goes off I want you to immediately drop what you are doing and make your way to the top deck. Do NOT stop to help a friend! The gas will replace all the breathable air down below in seconds. If you stop to help a friend I will have TWO dead assholes on my hands instead of ONE. If your friend drops, he is dead. Do NOT stop."

I thought that was pretty intense.

The food got worse by the day. Burgers and beans were becoming the meal de jour. I was having flashbacks of Korea. We ate burgers and beans sometimes twice a day for months while out in the field. My gums used to bleed back in those days. Could be, the thousands of gallons of alcohol I was consuming had something to with that, as well. Maybe?

I went for weeks on almost nothing but popcorn and hot chocolate. We had boxes of that shit. We could watch a movie at night in the cafeteria and that's when I'd feast.

We pulled into Singapore and resupplied and ate pretty good after that. It hurt though, as we sat in the harbor at Singapore and watched the town light up for two nights knowing we couldn't go ashore. A few of us had been around. We knew what we were missing. I swear it made me sick to my stomach. Thought about swimming the mile to shore but we'd probably need a tetanus shot by the time we got back the water was so filthy. Some of the most beautiful women in the world, only a mile away. Sigh.

We had to pass through some straits somewhere. The Captain called another formation.

"We are about to enter an area known for pirate activity. Yes, pirates. It might shock you to know that pirating on the high seas is alive and well. And they WILL attempt to board us even as a military vessel if they think they have a shot at overpowering us. We need to protect the ship."

All we had were our M-16s and night vision goggles. Fifty men to a side day and night for three days. Some pirates did come by. Two of them pulled up in a speedboat and parked about 75 feet away. Both wore ratty clothes and had submachine guns slung over their shoulders. There was also a 50 cal machine gun mounted to the deck on the nose of the boat. They had 50 rifles pointed at them so they just sat and watched as we sailed past. I was praying someone would get an itchy trigger finger just so there'd be something to do. No luck.

IT'S NOT THE HEAT; IT'S THE GOVERNMENT SUPPLIED CHLORINE AND PARASITES THAT GETS YA

It took six weeks to get to Bahrain. Then we spent six and a half months in the desert. This is the place where they grow all the hot for the world. It was around 130 when we got there. Oppressive heat. We were on an island so there was heavy humidity too. You'd think the sun would've burned it off but no.

The heat made you pass out and then it woke you up again because you were miserable. It was unbelievable. Tent city was enormous. Thousands of us in 12-man tents. The water supplied by the military was too heavily chlorinated so we mostly bought our water from the vendors on base. The chlorinated stuff gave us diarrhea. But then so did the cooks.

We got food poisoning four different times. It started when the cool weather set in. I woke up at 2 am needing to be on the can 5 minutes ago. It was now in the 30s at night. I put on boots and my winter coat and shorts and shuffled to the outhouses with my cheeks squeezed together as hard as possible. I get there to find about 1,000 other guys in the same predicament. It was taking too long so many were slipping off into the dark to go void out in the desert somewhere.

We had cramps and had to crap about 20 to 40 times a day. Each time it was like passing crushed glass out your backside. I actually developed an indentation on my knuckles where I would bite down before I released. It hurt so damn bad. Thankfully each bout would only last a week. Ha ha! That's a lot of BMs.

Todd flipped out one day over this. He was a little guy.

"I cannot keep shitting like this! I am gonna fucking evaporate!"

He went to medical and the doc handed him two pills. Then the doc got very serious.

"Listen carefully, son. Take ONE pill now and the other 12 hours from now and you'll be fine. Do NOT take both at once thinking you'll get better twice as fast. If you do, you will never shit again then you'll have a whole different problem on your hands."

Todd followed orders and was fine. The rest of us just toughed it out. It was a sign of weakness to go to medical.

KEN JENSEN

EVERY TEXAN I MET IN THE CORPS LOVED TO FIGHT, INCLUDING THE COMMANDER IN CHIEF. WE HAMMER IRAQ

I remember clearly when we were given the news that we had been ordered to attack. It was one of the heaviest moments of my life. It just wasn't real until I heard those words.

I stayed up to watch the first sortie fly out. It was 2 am. The birds were draped in bombs and missiles, way more than I'd ever seen mounted before. The wings on the jets were bent under the load. Also, I never saw more than 5 jets take off at a time in the past. This night there were close to a hundred. They took off one after the other in full afterburner. The noise was deafening. They formed a long, endless trail of flame in the sky, all headed north. Never before in my life had I ever become sexually excited from a non-sexual experience but tonight I literally had a rock hard-on!

Watching those jets take off en masse, carrying so much armament was incredible! I almost felt sorry for the enemy. This was the greatest display of impending death that I had ever witnessed. All I could think was, "Holy shit. A bunch of motherfuckers are gonna to die tonight. A bunch."

Soon after, I was in the chow tent having lunch with a Colonel. He was a pilot. Lots of ribbons on his chest. He looked tired.

"How's it going out there, sir?"

He looked at me before he spoke. He didn't look good. Weary.

"Son, I've been killing men for three wars now and it never bothered me before, beyond the obvious. But this war is too easy. It's like shooting fish in a fucking barrel." He truly looked sad.

He told me, "I was on a mission this morning. All I had to do was locate some generators, bomb them, and come home. As I cleared the horizon, the enemy spotted me and they all ran for cover. The whole unit jumped into the ditch where the generators were. I didn't want to kill anyone I didn't have to but I had my orders and my fuel was limited. I was actually screaming at them to get out of the ditch. I released my payload and climbed away. I never looked back. I felt like shit. But I had to watch the video of it when I got back to base for debriefing. It was like a fucking human tossed salad. Body parts everywhere."

I didn't say anything. What could I say?

KEN JENSEN

IDLE TIME BREEDS NEFARIOUSNESS

Day to day life during the war was mostly boring. There was a ton of work to get set up but once we were, it was business as usual. Just routine maintenance for the most part.

The boredom was crushing the heart out of me. But I managed to fit in some partying and a few evil deeds. I wasn't the only one.

Command had to literally send out an official order telling us to not drink windshield wiper fluid. Seems some guys somewhere were boiling it down and drinking the results in an attempt to get hammered. They all went blind.

I got some weed mailed to me that I hadn't requested. Just a gift from a friend. I got the whole tent high for two nights. It was a blast. We had just run out when another lunatic friend showed up with a small film canister.

"Guess what I just got in the mail today?" He was all excited until he saw our faces.

"You sons of bitches! You already had some and you didn't come get me?" He was pissed.

"War's hell, dude. Gotta stay on your toes or you'll miss all the fun."

Ken's note: I'm jumping ahead a little here but it proves the point of this chapter. Boredom is one of the military man's worst enemies. I was and still am, the type of person who loathes it more than most but it was a rough haul for all of us. As young men, we start to get into trouble if there's nothing constructive to do.

Once the war was over, the gear got priority over people. It all went home and we sat in the desert for two months, with absolutely nothing to do, just waiting for our freedom bird back to the States. That is prison time people. A lot went wrong for me during those two months.

WE WERE HONORED: THANK YOU USO

The USO did a few shows for us. One big one in particular was headlined by Bob Hope. To this day that is one of the coolest things that's ever happened in my life. Bob Hope performed for me in a war zone. Too fucking cool. Even better, he'd performed for my Grandpa in WWII fifty years prior. That made it ten times cooler. Me AND my Grandpa were entertained by Bob Hope while in a war zone!

Bob was hilarious. At this point in my life my favorite comedian was Sam Kinison. I saw him live three times. Whole other rack of stories. But Bob was special. I felt honored that he came to us. He'd think of something funny and actually have the cameramen shut down while he told us a dirty joke.

He would tell us, "Here's another great one I have to tell you but we can't record it."

He'd do the joke, we'd be floored because we were all used to the clean versions on TV and then he'd start up the cameras again. For what that whole experience was, you couldn't buy it man. You had to earn it.

Steve Martin came over too. The heat was kicking his ass big time. He was really sick. He wasn't allowed to do his normal routine for fear of offending our host nation. That always pissed me off. Our host nation would have been a parking lot if we hadn't shown up but I digress. Steve just had us come in close and he did nothing more than shoot the shit with us. And he was hilarious! He was just talking. Genius.

KENNY'S GONNA MURDER THE BOSS!!!

This little tale better illustrates where my head usually was at and what I was about as a Marine.

However I managed it, I got drunk earlier in the day. I was scheduled for generator watch that night at the shop. No biggie. Even wasted I could handle it. Got to the shop expecting a pleasant evening of dicking around and found the boss still at his desk.

I hated this guy. This was the third time in three countries and as many years, that he'd been our boss. He came and went over the years. He was "By the Book." We were "The Dirty Dozen." Some friction came of this.

As I went to and fro tending to minor tasks, I noticed he was eyeballing me. He knew what was up and he was playing mental chess of some sort with me. My rage grew inside me. I took as much as I could then let out three years worth of frustration on him the only way I could.

I went back to his desk and commenced hollering, cursing, and swearing, threatening his life, and punching every single thing in his office other than his head. That's the short version.

Palmy ran back to the tent and got the whole crew to come running and save me from a lengthy brig sentence.

"He's gonna fucking kill Goodie! I shit you not! You guys gotta help me stop him! He's completely outta control!"

Meanwhile, back at the Bat-shop: I laid it out clear, through tears of frustration. I was crying like a baby in between punches to every single metal surface I could find. If he hadn't already figured it out, I reiterated that I wanted nothing more than to kill him with my bare hands. He took it well. Seriously. The man was cool as a cucumber. I explained (in a roaring tone of voice) how I couldn't understand why I hadn't already killed him and that I was sick of his trying to cram the entire fucking Marine Corps codebook down our throats at every turn.

"Don't you get it!?" I screamed.

"You are trying to break us, mold us into your image. It ain't gonna fucking happen! We are the ANTI-versions of you and that's how it's gonna stay. You'll NEVER change us. You've been trying for three years! Guys run and try to look busy when you enter the shop. Fuck—that! If there's nothing to do—it's because EVERYTHING FUCKING WORKS BECAUSE WE'VE DONE OUR JOB RIGHT!!!"

"You're just a man and I'm not playing your game anymore. Fuck you."

The guys made it back to the shop just in time to hear the last little bit. They saw I was spent, the office dented and destroyed, but the boss was untouched. So they let me say my piece. I found out later that everyone thought I'd nailed it, I was funny while psychotic, and they were glad someone had finally spoken up.

The next day we had a shop meeting. By now, I was feeling a little foolish, humbled. Couldn't believe I'd cried. Shameful. But we were in for a surprise.

The boss said, "I had a very interesting meeting with Cpl. Jensen last night and he explained some things to me of which I was unaware. We're going to do things a little different from now on and I think you will all approve."

And here's the kicker. He actually, from that moment on, became one of the best bosses we'd ever had, and we grew to like him. Even me. Shoulda had that talk YEARS sooner.

HERE'S TO YER HEALTH

This was sweet. Who knows what the following may have done to me. We were ordered to get anthrax shots. Whatever. We went. Quick shot in the arm, same as the many dozens that had come before it. Having been overseas three times I was a veritable pincushion. I think I'm rated for just about any type of biological attack anyone could throw at us. It'll just be me and the cockroaches left standing.

Anyhow, within a few days we all developed these thick scabs on our shoulders. They grew to encompass the entire shoulder cap and when we rapped on them with our knuckles they sounded like wood. The injected arm hurt like hell. Even hurt when the wind blew across it. The arm was also useless during this time. Every color in the rainbow seeped out from under that scab.

Two weeks later we were ordered to go get the booster shot. Turnout was pretty lean for that round. Me and my guys got together and decided they could come for us with MPs. That was the only way we'd get injected. We weren't alone. Many guys didn't go and the issue wasn't forced.

Then someone decided we should start taking our nerve agent counteraction pills. For what? I'm still alive so I s'pose there's no nerve gas around. And what do we do if nerve gas does get launched at us later? We know our pills won't have been replaced in time.

Shit, they had an exercise before the war even began in which the whole unit had to don their charcoal NBC suits. Just so we could get a taste of what that might be like. Again, me and my guys found a place to hide and skipped the whole exercise. Result? About 500 wasted suits, expensive suits that were never replaced when the actual war kicked in. Only my shop still had suits.

We couldn't even get fucking MREs replaced quick enough! So my shop took a pass on the nerve agent thing as well. Glad we did. I heard some nasty stories from other vets years later as to what happened when they ate those pills for an extended period of time. See what I mean? Just didn't pay to follow each and every little order that came down the pike.

Ken's note: This read sort of light but I truly wonder what they did to me. I have about 40 inoculations in me from those five years alone. The Anthrax shot was experimental. If you dig deep enough into literature about vaccines, you'll find info that sheds light on possible side effects that is not ever told to you by any doctor. I only know so much about that, but I wonder.

THE TROUBLE WITH INBREEDING

I went to town and got blasted with TJ and a redneck associate from work. The redneck and I ended up in a brawl of his making when we got back to tent city. He was mad about a night I shared with him and his contract wife in Tijuana about Two years ago.

Some couples would marry just to get the supplemental paycheck for married individuals. They'd only see each other every two weeks at the bank to split the check. This asshole fell in love with his contract bride. Long story as are all stories that take place in Tijuana.

The only reason I didn't kill him was because I was too drunk to stay on my feet. He'd wanted to fight all night and I kept redirecting him. It finally became unavoidable. But once he fired me up he knew he was in trouble. So he kept punching me in the top of the head to keep me off balance. He told me later that he knew if I got my footing he was a dead man. Said I was growling and making noises he'd never heard a man make before. When I got mad it was otherworldly.

He bit a large chunk of meat out of the front of my shoulder. He also stomped one of my pinkies into the sand, breaking it in half. I did get him down eventually but I was too exhausted by then to do much damage. I settled for driving my thumbs into his eyes as deep as I could. I was in past the first knuckle. I wanted to pop his eyes and almost did but the little voice stopped me. Even insanely drunk, I knew it would be wrong to blind this moron. So I let him go.

By then, people broke us up. But my rage would not abate. Now I wanted to kill him. Couldn't blind him but murdering him somehow seemed just fine! I had my bayonet but someone took it from me.

I found him later and we began to wrestle. We fell into another unit's tent. We broke the big toe of some guy we landed on. Then we were broken up again. We were both in a spot of trouble the next day and we still had to work together but the moment was over. This stupid hayseed even thanked me the next day for letting him "work it all out."

"I feel great! Don't you?" he said. "And I'm glad you were so drunk that I stood a chance!"

Amazing.

Ken's note: This was the first time I truly and wholeheartedly wanted to murder someone. No guilt. As the next ten years of my life took place, I grew to feel it more and more in situations that required less and less provocation. Killing someone to get them out of my hair sounded more and more sensible the closer the illness came to the surface. Is this you? It's a signal! I hope you know that!

UNTIL YOU'VE PARTIED WITH A SHEIK YOU HAVEN'T REALLY PARTIED

Manama was interesting. It was an international stopover for businessmen from around the world. Many big hotels. Everywhere you went there were digital displays showing the current price of gold.

The Gold Souk was incredible. It looked like Fort Knox from the outside. Inside were at least five floors of small shops, side by side all selling gold. There were other doodads as well. I got burned on a deal but it was funny.

I bought a tin pipe that had wire braids wrapped around it, a huge smoking pot with a lid, a foot-long stem, and the middle had a birdcage-looking thing with dewdrops of tin dangling from it. It was one of the gaudiest things I'd ever seen. I had to have it. I paid $99 US for it. I thought it was some sort of Saudi heirloom type thing. Many years later, I would see the same exact pipe in a head shop in Denver, for 8 bucks. Same friggin' pipe! Go figure.

In the hotels you could drink. There were no bars per se but all the hotels had small bars in them. I sat with a sheik one night drinking Heinekens. The hotel bar was just out of hand. Big international party. My arm is over his shoulder and he could care less.

"Look Sheik. This will be rude of me but I will probably never have this chance again, so I'm just gonna ask, 'How much money DO you have?'"

He told me, "You do not have a word in English that represents that big of a number, my friend." The two of us shared a big laugh over that.

The Sheik and I got up together and went to the head.

I was just releasing my golden bounty when the Sheik informed me, "You must be careful, my friend. Some of the men in my country...they like...how you say...the little boys."

I stopped mid-stream and shot him a look of concern with a hint of danger.

He threw his hands up and said, "No, no, no, no, not *me*! I just say that some others will do this thing. You need to be careful in city. But not me!"

I had myself a hard laugh and resumed urinating.

"Don't worry, Sheik. I heard the rumors. I'll guard my tight end!"

Then *he* laughed and we went back to the bar.

Earlier we had been at the Navy base. I met sailors from Germany. They could not comprehend sailing halfway across the world with no beer on board.

They said they had enough beer that if the ocean dried up, they'd dump their beer overboard and it would be enough to float the rest of the way home. I hung out with Brits and I know a few other countries were represented at that party.

We had a HumVee and somehow we picked up a soldier who was AWOL from the mainland. He was amusing at first because he was plastered. That was why he snuck away. Had to have a drink. But as the night wore on he started getting dangerous. He had a knife, a .45 and a .22 pistol on him. My boss was driving and I told him what was up.

"Bob, we gotta dump this guy. He's wasted, looking for blood and armed to the teeth. Bad combo man. He's gonna get us in trouble."

My boss was a big boy. He got the ammo from the guy and later, we somehow ditched him.

The party with the Sheik wrapped up but we of course wanted to keep going. We made friends with a Norwegian war correspondent. We went to his room, ten of us, and he got a big box of airline bottles of booze brought up. Everything was going fine when I noticed we were missing two guys.

"Where's Matt and Palmy?"

"Went out the window," someone casually replied.

"Out the window?! We're ten fucking floors up! And there's no balconies on this building!"

"Whatever," came the reply.

I stuck my head out and there they were. Matt and Palmy were on a ledge, maybe 4 inches wide and sloped downward, with their arms spread wide gripping the wall. The wind was pretty strong and there wasn't much to hold on to.

"What the hell are you guys doing? You'll get killed!" I yelled.

They ignored my tone.

"Come on out, Ken! This fucking ROCKS!"

That was a sound enough argument for me. I went out and joined them. We enjoyed the view for a while, then decided we were probably pushing our luck and shimmied back inside.

Later we found the service elevator and went down to the sub basement and found some tunnels that took us all over the place. Near dawn, room service had put out breakfast for many of the rooms. We went through every floor and ate all the food we found. We were pretty hungry.

ZIGGED WHEN I SHOULDA ZAGGED

Ialways kicked myself for this night. I literally could have avoided what came next by taking a different turn in the road. I only wanted to go to the tent, read a book, and go to sleep. I heard voices that I recognized, on the other side of a shipping container I was nearing. I mentally flipped a coin on whether I should say hello or just go to the tent and pretend I didn't hear them. I chose to say hello and in doing so, I chose my doom.

I was offered some medical grade alcohol. 190 proof. Legal moonshine. Me and two other guys drank about a quart of this stuff. It was like inhaling fire. This night became extensively fucked up to include me threatening the biggest, strongest, and brawlingest guy in our unit, whom also happened to be our new boss, among many other things. I went on quite a tear through camp. I got busted again. This time just for being drunk. Against regs. The sad thing is four days later the regs changed but they wouldn't let me slide.

The powers that were got mad because I'd talked this guy into firing a round into the air with his M-16 in the middle of tent city. It was after we supposedly had turned in all our rounds. My friend had stashed some extras. So technically I got busted but then nothing happened. We got our bird back to the world and I carried on with life in El Toro without a hitch.

Ken's note: If this doesn't prove to you how the tiniest of decisions can lead to the most profound changes in one's life, nothing will. This was the ultimate example of "the flapping of a butterfly's wings in America causing a hurricane in India" that I'd ever experienced.

KEN JENSEN

HELL HATH NO FURY LIKE SHORT-TIMERS

During my final six months I made some new friends. These guys were more my speed. Very self-destructive, multiple busts, not afraid of much of anything, and hated being enlisted with a passion just like me. We were like three versions of the same guy. I spent the remainder of my enlistment with these two. Jaime and Dudu. We would become inseparable. We were fiercely loyal to each other and we each depended on the other two for moral support.

I somehow was able to ratchet up every bad thing in my life to a new level with this crew. Every single day something funny, twisted, violent, or illegal took place. We were out of control. I was running at max speed by now. We all wanted out so bad that we didn't want to remember each day as it happened.

We stayed blitzed on anything we could get our hands on. We went through a month-long intense coke spell. I almost killed the dealer at his home one night so we lost our connection. He said something to me that he shouldn't have. My guys pulled me off of him before the roughly one dozen knives aimed at me were sent home.

Smoked a lot of weed. Drank practically non-stop.

Went through a nightmarish huffing phase to include nitrous oxide, ether, Freon, and shoe polish. We'd sometimes do a string of nonstop huffs. Empty the lungs, inhale one substance, enjoy the ride, exhale. Then fill back up with the next inhalant, no fresh air, repeat until we'd sampled all we had on hand.

Funny thing, I found the shoe polish to offer the most pleasant high of almost anything I'd ever ingested. We all had something traumatic happen to us that made us quit the inhalants. Thank God.

We tripped on acid many times. Those nights are actually fond memories still. Those were some heavy times. We were hell bent on personal destruction. But we kept each other laughing.

Our mission in life (beyond staying fucked up) was to laugh as much as possible at all times. Jaime kind of tamed me and Dudu and kept us upbeat when we were down. We always considered him the happiest of the bunch. That very fact threw us when he later took a half-assed shot at suicide. Some slashing was involved but it wasn't serious enough to get the job done.

Dudu was the clown. He went out of his way constantly to turn even the smallest little nothing into a laugh attack. He'd say the sickest most perverse things with a completely straight face and nonchalant attitude.

I was the lunatic. I had to be watched by the other two more than I ever did the same for them. I would be the first to get angry about anything. I was the loosest cannon and I harbored the most ill will towards the rest of the human race compared to the other two.

All these roles could be interchanged amongst us as well. Depended on many variables. But I loved these guys. Intensely. We knew what we were about and we chose to revel in it. We were our own little three-man psycho support group.

I even managed to get thrown in jail again. Same damn jail I'd been in one year prior. This time I was picked up in a parking lot. Stumbling with intent to fall is how I put it. I wasn't charged and other than wandering drunk in public I hadn't done anything.

In the morning my friends were waiting for me. And how they found me was funny. Popeye (he had huge out of proportion forearms), a guy who was new to our group, had taken me with him to some town. I was just a tad inebriated when we left. He left me alone in the car to go look for a nearby party on foot. When he came back I was gone. That's all he knew. He looked for me briefly then gave up. The boys were not happy with him when he got back to the room.

"Whattaya mean 'you lost Kenny?!' How did you lose him?"

"I left him in the car while I looked for this party."

"You LEFT him in the car?! Alone?!"

"Yeah. Why?"

"You can't leave Kenny alone when he's drunk! He wanders! So let's do this: what town were you in when he disappeared?"

"Balboa Island."

"That's Newport Beach. That's where Kenny is. Newport Beach Jail."

It was that simple. They made one phone call and found me. That's how they were waiting for me in the morning. As I exited the jail I was received with open arms and much clapping of hands. It was a hoot! Just another day.

Out of all my time in the Corps, partying like I did, these 6 months were the most monstrous. I really don't know how we lived through it or retained any mental capabilities whatsoever.

Ken's note: Oh boy, did I glaze over this period! There are some things from this time, that don't need to be seen by the public eye. Like I said, I took my insanity and ran with it as an operating platform. This is how one avoids responsibility. It also is what happens when one is clueless as to how he can stop. It's a giving up, a giving in. I feel this was nothing more than slow suicide. I seriously left out a lot of shit. Madness is not pretty and this is all I felt like sharing.

SO CLOSE AND YET SO FAR AWAY

I was checking out of the Marines. You get a signoff sheet that needs about 70 signatures from anybody on base you may have unfinished business with. It takes a full week of solid running around to get this sheet filled in time. I'm at S-1, the paperwork division waiting for something to be done with my record book. In 7 days I will be a civilian. It is all I want and I want it bad. I want my freedom.

I wait in the hall for hours. Finally the Corporal calls me to the counter. He asks for my sign-out sheet. I hand it to him.

"Dude, I'm sorry. This ain't me but I'm under orders."

With that he rips my SEPS sheet in half.

"What the fuck are you doing?!" I yell at him.

"Man, we found your record book finally. It's on the Colonel's desk. You're up on office hours."

"For what?! I haven't pulled anything since I've been back from the Gulf!"

"That's it man. The Gulf. Some shit about a discharged firearm."

And so it went. I got put back into the service for another two and a half months just so I could serve my two hours of extra duty after work each day. Clean toilets and wax floors at Headquarters. The Colonel who handed out my sentence was new. I found out the last Colonel, whom I knew, was going to let me go but he transferred before I could be dealt with. The new guy was a born again Christian. Felt it was his moral and ethical duty to "teach this young Marine a valuable lesson."

I was out of control before this bust. Now I don't even know what category I became. My rage was immeasurable. I was psychotic. But what could I do? Quit that's what. I quit. I went to each morning muster so the boss would know I was alive, then I'd go back to the barracks until the next day. Brad was behind the scenes working with the new boss who wanted my ass.

Brad told him, "Staff that guy IS 990. He does it all. He has always loved this job and he's trained everybody in here including me. This shop would not even be what it is if not for how he built it. He's always been the hardest worker and he'll fight to the death with anyone who even speaks poorly about this shop. Just give him some room. He deserves it."

So they did. The bosses left me alone. Once I'd served my time I was free.

Ken's note: More glazing over. Until my security guard stretch, which was ten years away yet, this was the absolute darkest period of my life. I was dangerous. I was incredibly dangerous at this time. I lived with colossal rage. Even my friends handled me with kid gloves. I was Willy.

SO CLASS, WHAT DID WE LEARN FROM ALL THIS?

That was a good snapshot of my life in the Marines. But believe me, I left out hundreds of incredible stories. I'm not even exaggerating. Hundreds. I watered down many details as well. But all of that is for another book.

I make no apologies to anyone who may feel I wasn't a proper Marine. That to me is a relative term. I was one of the worst in some ways I suppose, but I had a lot of company over the years. I wasn't THAT different from many around me.

I did my job well and that's what I was there for. I volunteered to risk my life for my country. And my life was risked. Me and the Corps are even as far as I'm concerned.

I searched out adventure, violence, comedy, the odd, and the better high the whole time I was in. The nature of my shop allowed me to get away with more than most. My friends and I were not typical. We knew this and strived to keep it that way for better or for worse. During times of peace, guys like us would have just been kicked out. So in one respect, I got lucky.

I shared what I thought would display the path to my bipolar disorder the clearest. My Marine life played a massive part in building me into all that I became, both good and bad. It still directs my path in certain ways today. Once a Marine, always a Marine.

It wasn't all bleak or even violent or illegal. I always said when it was good it was better than I could ever have conceived possible. But when it was bad the same held true.

The good times were so good that I wouldn't trade them for anything. Even knowing that most of my behavior had a big part in breaking me down later in life. I'm still close friends with a group of these guys.

But I could never truly tolerate the lack of freedom my military contract imposed on me. I was often homesick or lonely. I fought depression a lot more than those around me even knew. I just hid it under a veneer of psychosis. I knew I was doing this but it was a survival issue for my mind. I built up this crazy persona to help me deal with the areas of myself that I felt lacked strength. Somewhere along the line I actually became that person.

The longer I was in the less I wanted to remember each passing day. Because of this I probably blacked out around fifty times in my last six months alone. I wanted time to speed up. Overall, I blacked out hundreds of times. For all I've written and all I the stuff I have written down elsewhere, there is much I can't recall.

As I wrote this book, Big T called me and reminded me of the morning in the Gulf when I awoke him with my bayonet pushed up against his windpipe.

I whispered, "TTTTT-JJJJJJ," softly, until he opened his eyes, felt the knife at his throat, and looked into my grinning face.

"Wake up fucker! It's time for breakfast!"

The next day he woke me up by thrusting his bayonet, mounted on his M-16, into my cot all around my head, hairs away from slicing my face.

"YOU wake up fucker! I'm hungry!"

I barely remember that. Wish it was clearer. That is some funny shit!

I did learn something important though. I knew beyond a shadow of a doubt that as soon as I got out I would have to quit drinking for good. And I did. For the next seven years anyway.

I had to smoke a lot of weed to keep myself from drinking. I really didn't care that I'd only replaced one with the other. Paramount to me was simply NOT drinking.

I continued to trip and shroom whenever possible as I really enjoyed the hell out of those two things. I really had no intention of quitting them. But up to this point, drugs had never brought me any negativity. I didn't do anything stupid or break the law in any way comparable to the shit I pulled when drunk. The drinking only brought me pain. Drugs still kept me happy. That didn't last.

When I first got home I remember having a talk with my father because I felt he just wasn't truly understanding the nature of the dilemma I faced. I was perpetually miserable and angry. I told him I thought I'd damaged my natural ability to ever be happy again. I knew this was a very real possibility.

The booze replaces the happy hormones in your head. Same with drugs. Drink long enough and your body sees no need to make any on its own. Then if you quit drinking your body no longer knows how to make the happy juice anymore. You're sober but you're left with a hole in your personality. Now you're never happy for any reason.

I was miserable for months. I had no joy in me. I could laugh at comedies but it wasn't a lasting effect. It was a double whammy because although I was happy to be a free man again, it felt as if I'd lost my protector status and been thrown back into the herd, stripped of my honor. That's just how it was.

It took almost a year for me to feel naturally happy again. I usually just felt anger. That was partly another defense in itself. It was easier for me to be angry than it was to be nice. Kept people the fuck away from me. It was a way to isolate myself. Being an asshole is simpler than being a boy scout.

But truly, I could no longer feel joy for any reason. This became a cruel existence. My only thoughts were not to drink. Mentally, emotionally, I was crippled.

THE DARK LORD'S CHILD IS AWAKENED: MY FUTURE ILLNESS TAKES ROOT

I THOUGHT I WAS HAPPY:
MORE SELF-DECEPTION

The only thing I did that was good for me was lifting weights. I started when I was 14 and I continued until my bipolar disorder and various other life problems shut down my drive and ability to lift. I suffered a two-year layoff. I never competed but lifting made me feel like a champ so without it I was very unhappy. But thankfully I got to a place where I could do it again. I hope I never stop.

During my smoking years I used to tell people that I was the healthiest hippy they'd ever meet. I swam outdoors, hiked, camped, rock climbed, and did most of it while high or tripping. For a while it was perfect. Got to have my cake and eat it too. I would come to learn I'd only been fooling myself. All the pot smoking and tripping brought on my bipolar disorder much faster than it would have occurred naturally. I'm sure of that. But I did have a really good time there for a while.

I met a friend through my brother. They'd had quite the history together. This new friend was in the same boat as I; couldn't drink but loved the weed and the hits. Also was a big fan of the outdoors. We were a perfect match. The two of us had some massively entertaining moments in the great outdoors. We had the same style of wit and the same sense of humor. A word or glance from one would be enough to set the other to choking with laughter. But over time even this fell apart. We never discussed this rift. It just sort of happened.

I started seeing how my partying was getting me nowhere but my friend figured he'd just go at it even harder. I believe my mood started changing for the worse around now as well. Nothing dramatic. Just little signals of the storm to come.

KEN JENSEN

I FIND TRUE LOVE. IT SAID SO RIGHT ON THE MARRIAGE CERTIFICATE

Soon after I met my first wife. She was from Queens and was the very embodiment of the borough. Total attitude. She was also very smart and cosmopolitan. She was responsible for my second awakening. Just opened my eyes to a piece of the world I'd been overlooking. We could make each other laugh too. She had a biting wit and razor sharp sarcasm. We had a lot of good times.

The story of how I met her is a fine example of the power of the mind. I had only been home about 7 or 8 months and had been sober for that length of time as well. Without drinking I didn't know how to get a girl. I didn't know how straight people pulled it off. So I developed a simple plan. I would lift weights constantly, work outside on the yard in nothing but shorts and hope some girl on vacation visiting her family would spot me and take interest. It's kooky. That is exactly how I found her. Her aunt and uncle lived right across the street. It's even more profound because my tiny little town is in the middle of nowhere. I had the Universe helping me with this one.

She eventually proposed to me via ultimatum. I agreed out of defeat. I didn't want to marry her but I wanted to be alone even less. Went so far as to sell my Harley to pay for her wedding ring. I folded like a cheap house of cards under the onslaught of her one demand.

KEN JENSEN

CHASING THE DREAM, FINDING ONLY PAIN

We moved to Denver out of compromise. I wanted woods and she wanted city. It was all downhill from there. Prior to Denver we'd never really lived together. Our schedules kept us apart. We didn't really see each other until the weekend. It was like that for almost 5 years.

We found that being together all day was not working well for us. We both liked to do totally different things with our day. We couldn't enjoy doing things together and neither would budge. We fought like demons in the normal course of a day. We had an explosive relationship but all verbal. We'd been that way for so long we thought it was normal. We scared the shit out of tamer people. The arguing intensified once we were on the same sleep schedule.

I got fed up with work and began a massive job-hopping campaign. I would eventually hold over twenty jobs in less than three years. At the same time, the bipolar was starting to surface. I didn't know it then but it's easy to spot in retrospect. I began to loathe being an employee. I wasn't afraid of hard work, as I'd done it all my life. It was the futility of holding a job that would stagnate and never bring me what I wanted in this life that got me. I had an epiphany not long after reaching Denver.

I had just returned home in my work truck. The day had been brutal both physically and mentally. I was exhausted in a deep, deep way. Then it hit me: I can NOT keep doing this! I have to do my own thing! I was never the same from that point forward. Working for someone else would just get harder and harder and harder for me to tolerate. It literally started to drive me crazy.

Right around now is when my future Amway sponsor met me. I could write a book just on this dark period of my life. I tried intensely for almost three years to make that program work. I didn't like it for the same reason most people don't but I thought if I could just get people to listen to me and sign up, I'd run the show my way. A way that would be satisfying to people. Of course this didn't pan out.

I have a very dim view of that company and its system but I'll just say I'm glad I'm out. But imagine this: My panic attacks began while I was trying to prospect strangers. I'm trying to meet people, conjure up some bullshit reason to talk to them, and somehow get their personal info in a way that arouses no suspicions, so I can later show them my secret business plan, while deflecting any questions as to my real purpose, WHILE experiencing a panic attack! It was like living through a mini stroke 5 or 6 times a week.

And even though I tried to avoid it, I became the guy people fear. I prospected everyone! I had no idea how so many people could not see the simplistic beauty of this business plan. I just wanted to be rich and figured many others wanted the same thing. This is when my manic side began to show. I moved on to other projects.

I had huge visions of my grand future. I did not acknowledge failure even as it was happening. I went through a slew of companies online and off trying to make enough money to work from home. My marriage was disintegrating. I smoked weed the whole time and I began to drink very occasionally too as my stress levels climbed higher and higher. I spent money we didn't have. She did the same but I viewed her purchases as bad decisions. My decisions were gonna make us rich. Couldn't she see that? Shit. It was truly an insane time.

LIFT 'TIL YOU PUKE!

Not all was blue. I joined a hardcore gym outside of Denver. The owner was always smiling and hollering "Huge!" at me when I came in. It was a second home to me. Everyone was for real in this place. Lots of blue-collar types. Lots of big dudes.

The gym was on the small side. It had three main rooms with equipment divvied up by body part. A mix of old and new equipment. Shitloads of plates. In this gym everyone moved a lot of metal so plate trees were everywhere. The stereo system was always set to a hard rock/heavy metal station and blasting. If the crowd was light you could bring in your own music and hear whatever you wanted.

The stench of sweat was detectable from the parking lot even though the gym was two floors up. There was one window a/c. It was in the leg room where it was most needed. I would lose water by the gallon in sweat during summer. Often as I came in there'd be someone staggering down the stairs barely able to walk after leg day. I frequently left the same way. The atmosphere in this place was fairly intense. We were all there for one reason—to get huge. As my symptoms began to kick in the gym would alleviate some of them.

Ken's note: I felt it important to show you this so you could see where my mind was headed. I thrived in Jeff's gym and it was because of the uber-intense atmosphere. This was a warrior's arena and it matched my internal fire. Lot of nice guys but downright bloodthirsty about getting huge and strong. You had to be accepted by the group as someone who deserved to train there. This was unspoken but crystal clear on everyone's face. Nobody messed around when it came to training. The whole gym was Alpha Male. Even the chicks.

KEN JENSEN

HARDCORE TRAINING INVOLVES BLOOD

One day I was seated on the end of a bench doing alternating dumbbell curls. Jeff, the owner, walked over and yelled, "What's this?!"

I looked down and there was a pool of blood on the floor under my right hand.

Four days prior I had been replacing a pin punch in a machine press. I was doing it all wrong because it was 5:30 AM and I was tired and hated my job. HATED it! Tried to line up the punch as it went into the hole. Many tons of force. The pin caught the edge of the hole and the hardened steel exploded into my hand, which had been guiding it in. I felt the shock and the recognizable sensation that comes from a pressure wound. I knew I'd just fucked up good.

Blew a hole in my hand that required 5 stitches to close. I had waited four days before attempting to lift so that it could close up. I couldn't wait any longer. It was time to lift. The surface had healed but not the interior. I was bleeding profusely. I apologized to Jeff and explained what happened. I told him I'd clean it up right away.

"Fuck that! That's what I love about you! You even lift when you're injured! You will lift until you bleed! That's awesome! Fling it on the mirrors! Get it all over the place! Let people know what kind of gym I run!"

And it was that kind of a gym too.

KEN JENSEN

TRAIN 'TIL YOU DIE

There was one brute who never talked to me when I said hello. After a few months I stopped trying. It was just weird because the place was so small. This guy was unbelievably strong. He never smiled. He looked like something out of a Conan book.

Maybe a year goes by and I'm alone with him in one room. I'm resting between sets of deadlifts and he's just gearing up. He looks up at me and begins talking as if he's picking up where we left off last. I don't want to upset him so I pay attention.

He starts telling me that he's had four heart attacks and some strokes and how he USED to be strong! He tells me how he went to Mexico and bought something in a pharmacy that he'd heard would make him stronger. He got home and began injecting himself. For two weeks he got very strong then tapered off, then began feeling weak and sick. He kept lifting, because he was an unstoppable force of nature and kept injecting.

Someone convinced him to go to a doctor and he felt bad enough to go. Doc drew some blood and came back with the good news.

"I've isolated the stuff you're taking and I can't identify what it is but when I look through the scope I see it is attacking and killing your red blood cells. Don't take one more shot or I believe you will die."

"So I stopped taking that shit," he tells me all nonchalant.

Next he tells me of a late night walk to his car in a parking garage. He feels a pain in his chest that is so bad he has to lean up against the wall in the skier's position. The pain is the worst he's ever felt and he's close to blacking out but he stays alert. It lasts twenty minutes and no one shows up to help him. It eventually passes and he gets in his car, goes home and thinks nothing of it. In talking to his wife, WEEKS later, she convinces him to get a checkup.

After the tests the doc says, "You have had what we in the industry refer to as a 'Widow Maker.' It is the worst kind of heart attack you can have and is usually fatal. It also causes the most pain possible and you are telling me that you just stood against a wall and TOOK IT? You shouldn't even be here my friend. I'm talking to a ghost."

"Ain't that somethin'?" my new friend asks.

And that was it. We both went back to lifting. He turned out to be one of the nicest guys I ever met. He just was damned serious when he was in the gym.

I met him and his wife once in a store. She told me I should've seen him when he was big.

"Head looked like a pimple down between his shoulders!"

LIFE STEALS MY LOLLIPOP

I could always count on the gym to make me feel better. I lived for the rush of adrenaline. The mastery of pain. It gave me a sense of accomplishment. There was a brotherhood here. The edgy atmosphere maintained by all matched how I normally felt. But I began experiencing some freaky sensations on my rides home after lifting.

As I drove I would get the feeling that my being was no longer centered in my body but rather a foot above my head and to the left. Conscious out of body experiences. This was scary enough in its own right but I was going 65 mph down the road in a car and I couldn't feel my body! Couldn't feel the wheel in my hands or the pedals at my feet. This would last a minute or two and I'd start to re-center. I really don't know how I kept the car on the road. It was incredibly scary and disorienting.

As my life fell apart all around me, I noticed I could not focus on the task in hand while lifting. Right in the middle of a set I'd start thinking about my lack of money, my shitty job, my bad relationship with my wife, etc. Negative mania was setting in. This was an unsafe situation as I would sometimes be involved with a large amount of weight. I could blow a joint or wreck my back or get crushed depending on what I was doing.

I had to take a break from the gym for a couple months. I found through research that lactic acid, which you are full of after lifting, is a direct antagonizer of bipolar symptoms. I was lifting to feel better but the lifting was now causing me to come unglued in my mind. Great.

I would also learn, years later, that severe exercise really screws with your meds and causes symptoms to intensify. I'm sure this very thing was also taking place in my body. I lifted like the Sun was gonna go Nova any second. I had heart.

THE BEST RIDE IN THE PARK

B y now I was beginning to exhibit the classic symptoms of extreme lows and highs. The severity of the symptoms grew worse in a short amount of time. The mania that I wasn't even aware that I'd had was fueling my "Big Idea" moments and costing me a fortune. I chased down anything that looked like it would bring easy money through working from home. That particular list is shamefully enormous.

I was walking off of jobs. I attempted and quit a large number of jobs trying to find something that I found both enjoyable and provided the amount of income I needed. I was finding it didn't exist. I started accepting shit jobs to avoid the heavy responsibilities I normally faced but quitting them out of disgust because I wasn't using my skills and talents.

I could do almost anything I tried and was usually good at it but due to dissatisfaction I'd soon quit. I rebuilt my resume for each interview to say what I needed it to and not many references were ever checked. Even though I quit jobs constantly I was never out of work long.

I started having apocalyptic dreams. God would be in his robes, all hair and beard and Old Testament-like, standing behind an impossibly tall altar looking down upon me in judgment. And I wasn't faring well with him. Too many wrongs, not enough rights. I'd then wake up racked with terror, heart pounding far, far too hard in my chest, body numb, feeling as if I couldn't breathe and was close to the brink of insanity with the fear of death.

Oh, how I feared death and dying. It crushed me. I never realized your mind was capable of producing such a level of fear and anguish. Because my body was numb I would be running all around the apartment beating my limbs against the walls and furniture trying to regain any level of sensation. While wrapped in that terror I just described. Fun, fun, fun!

I felt like no matter how hard I inhaled, my lungs simply could not get enough oxygen. I sat around constantly deep breathing but never feeling satiated in my oxygen needs. It was like perpetual drowning. All this breathing would then cause hyperventilation with its own set of uncomfortable conditions. I would learn that this is also a classic symptom.

I also experienced symptoms after a meal or any time when I became too hungry. I'd get panicky. No doctor ever had an explanation for this or knew of it from some other patient. I have since assumed that any change in hormone or nutrient level in my body is enough to throw off whatever is holding my mind together normally. Run out of food or put some in—either way—tragic system-wide hyper response for me. Knowing I was seemingly the only person to experience this scared the shit out of me even more.

Then came the depression. Manic was bad and caused me to do stupid things but it didn't feel bad. The depression was excruciatingly bad. I would often end up in the fetal position on the couch or floor certain that nothing I ever did or could possibly think to do would be good enough to allow me to survive, let alone prosper.

I'd been pretty damned depressed in the past. I even had times where I couldn't bear to look at my own reflection due to self-loathing. But this was far worse. It was so, so much worse. It paralleled the fear in its cataclysmic proportions. And sometimes, maybe an hour later, I would be King of the World, top o' my game. What the hell was wrong with me an hour ago? Who knows but I'm good now. I would cycle back and forth in the same day sometimes multiple times in one day. Then it got worse.

FEAR, INC.

I started secretly drinking again searching for relief from something I couldn't understand. I knew with crystal clarity that drinking only brought me pain but I sensed it was the only thing that might dampen these feelings in my head. I disappeared one night and didn't come home 'til dawn. The wife was frantic. I hadn't done anything stupid so I thought I was OK. Later that night I was smoking my bong to heal from the hangover. Then something new took place.

I felt a weird sensation building in my chest and spreading down my limbs. It was getting stronger by the second and I sensed it was gonna be very bad. Life altering bad. I was correct. My body felt as if it had its own black hole. It was collapsing in on itself in an impossible perpetual fashion. I felt as if I was disappearing into myself. It was horrifying.

At the same time my brain amped up. It seemed to be full of energy and baseless thoughts that went nowhere but kept coming at an incomprehensible rate. My brain spilleth over.

Then the fear hit me. It made the night terrors pale in comparison. This was cosmic. It grew exponentially. It was all consuming. I knew that I was going to die but not before I went horribly insane first. It kept growing.

Soon I was on all fours praying, begging God to make it stop. I'd do anything to make this stop. But I knew He wouldn't. Not his deal. This was something just about me. I was on my own. It was too funny. I didn't even go to church but there are no Atheists in foxholes right?

I told my wife to call an ambulance because I was freaking out and didn't know why. I kept it together until the ambulance arrived. I don't know how. Unfortunately a squad car and a ladder truck arrived as well. This was too fucking much. I needed an ambulance not a circus. It was overwhelming and embarrassing. I was still getting worse.

The EMTs hooked me into a monitor and injected me with something. When my numbers climbed past 200+ over 200+ I stopped watching. I knew it was just a matter of time before my heart exploded. I wished I could black out but I stayed conscious and aware throughout.

They gave me another injection on the way to the hospital. These shots had zero effect on me. Once in the ER I was injected with something more powerful. Nothing. My heart would not slow down. My fear would not abate. I was gettin' my money's worth out of this ride. I hollered for more. The doctor says I already have enough in me to drop a bull elephant. I tell him it's having no effect.

A tech jumped in. "He's right. Heart's not slowing down at all."

The doc said, "Fuck it. Let's give him this."

Whatever that last item was, it knocked me out. When I gained consciousness some hours later, all the nurses were giving me dirty stares. They knew I'd been drinking hard the night before and smoking weed today. So I was an addict and a loser in their eyes. Real nice of them. I found out my electrolytes had been far too low and other than that nobody knew what really happened to me.

I left the hospital with no explanation for what had caused any of it. I had another smaller attack the very next night. I discovered right away that it felt better if I kept moving so I took a walk. I headed towards the hospital. Stood across the street from it for over an hour waiting to see if I was gonna lose it or if I could maintain. I maintained and went back home.

A few days later I was back in the ER. I had the fear again but it wasn't as severe. I sat in the waiting room for three hours until a doc could see me. I was bugging out the entire three hours. Right here is when a new chapter opened in my life. One in which I was afraid to ever be farther than a mile away from any hospital at any time. I knew that only an ER had the stuff to slow my heart down and stop the fear and that I would never be given anything that strong to keep in my house.

PSYCHOS "R" US GETS A NEW CHAPTER MEMBER

Everything was coming to a point. We were sliding deeper into debt. We finally declared bankruptcy at the $72,000 mark. My stress levels kept rising. During a visit to my regular doc I requested some Valium, which he'd given me before. He detected a pattern. He wanted to know what was going wrong with my life. I told him that all I knew was that I was running out of tolerance for dealing with any further shit in my life and my life seemed to be turning all to shit. He gave me a thorough exam and said I was one of the healthiest patients he had, which led him to correctly believe that my problem was between my ears. He asked if I had a problem with seeing a psychiatrist and I said no, I just wanted to feel better.

My new psych quickly labeled me as classic bipolar. Then he dropped a bomb on me.

"Do you smoke a lot of weed?"

"Yeah."

"Do you do it to relax?"

"Yeah."

"Well, you're gonna love this. The weed is pushing you over the edge. It's *causing* your symptoms. Want to feel better fast? Stop smoking."

Shit. That sucked to find out. He gave me a book about bipolar and in it was a list of agitators. THC was the last item on the list.

"It's the last but it's a strong one."

Then he tells me, "The Valium you've been taking? With your problem that's like pissing on a house fire. You are way beyond Valium."

And so began the search for relief via pharmaceuticals.

THE HAT TRICK: PILLS, BOOZE, AND DIVORCE

Now I knew what was wrong with me as far as what to call it but I didn't really know what to do about it, how to fix it, whatever. I just did what the doctors told me to do. Well, this didn't work so well with the first guy. So I switched to the VA.

I saw a walking, talking computer of a psychiatrist whose only job was to okay whatever new drugs the psychologist recommended. We tried many, many drugs. Nothing worked well or for long. Consequently I began to drink a little more.

This led to a whole other area of problems. Of course it made everything worse. But I was becoming desperate for relief. The doctor seemed to be failing me as I saw it. But to be fair, nothing in my life was making me happy. All was stress. I had no joy only suffering. There were a few reasons for this. But the biggest was my marriage.

We didn't want the same things in life or even day to day. We had a talk on the morning following my last binge and ended it. It was painful but mutual. I admitted that I married her only because I didn't have the courage to say no. She admitted she had just wanted to see if she could tame me. We loved each other but not enough. So we split.

I learned that as much as we didn't belong together I missed her. The sense of loss I felt towards her was like a lead coat hanging from my shoulders. It felt like a physical pressure. I enjoyed my freedom but hated being alone. I got a new apartment and she would visit me with some regularity because she still worried about me. She really tried hard to help me be okay.

PLEASE, PLEASE, PLEASE, COMMIT ME!

My brother moved in with me some time later. I had a new job repairing gas station electronics, computers, and mechanical systems. I was on call every fourth day. That could turn into a 36-hour day sometimes. I drove around 500 miles a day servicing gas stations all over Colorado and the nearby states. The amount of information I had to learn to do this was staggering. I was doing it and doing it well but the pace was killing me.

Things weren't working with having a roommate either. I spent a whole day at a bar with my brother and we had a blast until the switch in my head flipped on. I literally thought he was the Devil. Crazy. We had a wrestling match in a street. He threw me to the ground right into a manhole lid. Separated the tendon between my shoulder and collarbone. That was excruciating. I thought my shoulder was broken. One X-ray later I found that I'd stretched that tendon as far as possible without tearing it. Normally, it is invisible in an X-ray. Mine was three quarters of an inch long. It eventually healed but my collarbone sticks up higher on that side now.

Then we returned to the apartment and had an official brawl. Smashed mirrors, big holes in the walls, furniture overturned. We did it up right. I was pretty ashamed of myself the next day but my brother was nonplussed. Chipper even.

"Yeah, we really threw down last night. It was awesome!" Well, at least I hadn't upset him.

I suffered another breakdown after that night and actually went to the VA to see if I could get committed. I felt like I was losing my mind. I needed a break. They wouldn't admit me. Said they had nothing for me. Now I was really at a loss. I met my wife later that day and she sent me home. Back east that is.

"You gotta go home to your mother. She's the only one who can help you. Keep seeing the doctor at the VA in New York. Get help!"

Then she bought me a used car with cash from a bonus she'd just received and I drove myself cross-country to New York. Thankfully there were no incidents on the trip home. I have to repeat the fact that my first wife did everything she possibly could to help me feel better. She still worries about me to this day. We couldn't be married but we were always great friends. I'm happy that it is still that way.

REALLY NOT DIGGIN' THE SYSTEM'S RESPONSE

I got home and the very next day went to the VA to get admitted to their psych ward. I figured that was where I needed to be. I was completely helpless at this time. I was in Hell and just seemed to be getting worse. I wanted relief so bad and was afraid it wasn't to be had. I was told that as bad as I was, I wasn't bad enough to get admitted. That really put things in perspective.

I realized there were people who were in worse shape than I was. I couldn't fathom feeling worse than I already did. I pity anybody who ever fell farther into the pit than I did. But I was pretty deep into it myself. Knowing someone else felt worse didn't alleviate any of the pain I was feeling.

I began working with a new doctor at the VA. We tried a lot of different drugs. Same results. I learned that I was now considered "mixed bipolar." I could be buried in depression while simultaneously being assaulted with mindless data my own head cooked up. I was fairly miserable and panic could hit at any time even with the meds. Nothing seemed to dampen my symptoms for long.

I would sometimes walk around the house for hours with the cordless phone in my hand, experiencing a panic attack, finger poised to dial 911, wondering if I should just get the hell into the ER. I couldn't work for months. I didn't do anything but sit at home and smoke cigarettes and talk to my mom. She was a great sounding board. I wouldn't get better for another five years from here but a lot of why I did is because she listened to me and had the patience of a saint. She allowed me the opportunity to talk it all out. I would find my own answers this way.

KEN JENSEN

BECOME A SECURITY GUARD AND SEE THE UNSEEN WORLD!

Eventually I got back to work. I couldn't tolerate the thought of repairing anything anymore so I became a security guard. It was a severe blow to my ego to climb those stairs to that office and then appear eager over the thought of fulfilling my dream to be a security guard. I really hated my life at that moment.

I got placed in a hospital. I was to specifically handle the ER on the overnights from Thursday to Sunday. This is when the most shit hit the fan. I called it the party hours. The work was fascinating. I saw just about everything you could imagine both psychological and physical. I truly loved this job. The irony of it was that I handled many, many people who had what I had. I was forced to fight the majority of these folks. The people I guarded were flight risks or wanted to hurt others or themselves or were just out of their minds, therefore out of control.

I had a motto I shared with anyone new. "We never limp to our cars and we never lose."

I told everyone who worked with me, "They don't pay us enough to get hurt. We don't even have benefits. If you got to hurt somebody to keep from getting hurt, then fucking hurt 'em. Also, I have a rep on the streets and with the cops. I don't lose. People know to behave when they come in here. If not, then I put it on 'em. Don't do anything that makes the guards look bad."

In truth, I was a little psychotic on this job. OK, probably a LOT psychotic. But when four cops drag in one man and then leave…well, I took steps to make sure my point got across. I was <u>one</u> guy but the <u>wrong</u> one guy to fuck with. I can't even share a lot of what I did and saw. But oh my goodness, what a fun time!

I also had to hold down violent people who were wounded, some terribly, but still combative, so the doctors could work on them or even begin to. I was right in the middle of everything. It was a blast! My face was right next to shit you only see on TLC or the Discovery Channel. This was not a normal security guard job and once the staff realized I wasn't the average retarded guard I was allowed to help more and over time, even expected to. It really was one of the best times of my life as far as work went.

KEN JENSEN

KENNY! YOUR PEOPLE NEED YOU!

I started getting a little bored after awhile. Not everybody was a fight and I found that if I handled myself a certain way, I could avoid fights. I also started talking to the patients more. Legally, I was not supposed to do that. I was supposed to just stand there and react if they lost it or keep them from trying to escape thereby putting the hospital in liability risk. But people do not like some uniformed goon just staring at them silently when they're feeling their worst. My presence made things worse. Escalation we called it.

So I talked. I adapted myself to wherever they were in their mind and acted accordingly. I handled it all: psychotics, overdoses, drunks, suicides, bipolar, schizos, bad trips, you name it. I'd enter their little world of pain and confusion and apply the soothing balm of my voice and caring ways. I empathized with a lot of them.

I saw how the system handled them and I was not happy. I used to demand better and faster care for "my people" as I called them. Hell, that's even what the staff started to call them after awhile. It became clear to all that I had a knack for dealing with crazy people and even though it was against the rules, it became expected of me.

Sometimes I'd even get the cops out faster than they wanted so I could help someone calm down. I expedited a lot of situations for the sake of the mentally ill. My judgment became accepted by the staff as well. If I said such and such had to happen in such and such a time, it usually got done. I was a great advocate for those of us teetering on the precipice of doom.

LIVING THE AMERICAN DREAM—SORT OF

It was at this job that I met my second wife. Again, another startling look into the power of the mind. Seems the Universe and I communicated well when I wanted a woman. Every time I saw her I thought the same thing. I can't share that thing with you but it was a happy thought. And it came true. It also brought about the birth of my first son.

She and I didn't match in all the ways we should and I tried to break it off. But when my son's imminent arrival became known I did what I felt was the honorable thing. We got married. I'll say this: we had a lot of great times in the beginning and a few sprinkled here and there later on but the relationship was a disaster. We were like oil and water. But we tried, I tried.

The stress of this marriage, the new son, and the three new stepchildren I also gained was becoming too much. We got dragged through the mud in a custody case with one of my stepson's father that was a complete nightmare. It lasted two years and the whole time I was filled with a hatred and rage for this other guy that was beyond description. I had my reasons believe me. The toll this took on both of us was unreal. Then we bought a house and two new cars. Looked like it might work out there for a little bit but then it didn't. My head got way worse.

KEN JENSEN

NEW DOC, NEW PILLS, NEW JOB, SAME RESULTS

I got fed up with the VA and switched to a local civilian doctor. I tried everything under the sun while with this man. He taught me about many more types of drugs I'd not heard of before. It gave me hope but it was short-lived. Nothing new worked either. In my infinite wisdom I began to drink yet again.

I got a DWI somewhere in here. I wasn't even in the car but it was parked next to the house whose door I was trying to kick in. Why? Not sure. I do know it involved a reality that only existed in my mind and that I scared the crap out of the poor woman who lived there. I felt like a real chump after that. I also got fired from the security job. The medical laws were being reinstituted and suddenly many of my tactics for subduing people were no longer acceptable. I was out.

I got a new job at a spinal and head injury center. I loved this job as well. These people needed our help for almost every aspect of their day. I enjoyed helping them immensely. I worked a crazy amount of overtime and it looked like I might be able to keep up with my bills. Then I got fired from there. This time there was no reason given.

AN OLD FRIEND SAYS GOODBYE / THE WATER'S CIRCLING THE DRAIN

Then my sex drive vanished. This scared the shit out of me. It was never in my life not present.

It's a shitty cliché "It happens to all men at some time. Yeah, but not me."

I had found a new wondrous torment. Sex was the only thing I knew would make me feel better if only for a little while. There's even more to it than that. Turns out that one of the major symptoms of bipolar disorder is an increased sex drive. And I did, in fact, want it all the time. Unfortunately, it was the cornerstone of our marriage too. Can you see the problem this would present me/us?

It was also a huge part of who I was. Appealing to the type of women who found me appealing was…appealing. I loved it! Now I'd lost it. And when it happened I had a big sense that it was gone for good.

I literally felt the urge in me die in my hand one night and I knew that "Elvis had left the building." It didn't leave me forever, thank God, but it was gone for almost a year and a half. That did wonders for the relationship. I knew that the illness itself was part of this. The stress in my life was outrageous and that definitely didn't help but I was on many meds and the side effect of some of them was loss of sex drive. This would prove to play a critical part in a bigger decision yet to come.

FLUSH!

Then came the day that changed everything. I went out and got wasted. I came home and was very mad at my wife and my life. Everything sucked. As a form of self-punishment I believe, and a way to piss off my wife, I ate a whole month's worth of Lithium. This landed me in a two-week-long coma. By all rights I shouldn't have lived.

It was a nightmare for my family, who had to witness me in the bed with all the tubes and machines keeping me alive. I paid for that in my heart for a long time. I was either unconscious or numb through all of it so I never felt much about it at the time. But I knew I'd destroyed my loved ones through worry. That's the beauty of bipolar disorder and the faulty decision making process that comes with it. You don't suffer alone. You take along everyone who cares about you too. Splendid!

I had death dreams again. These weren't so clear to me as the first one was when I was 15. And there were more of them. Basically I was involved in a lot of fights in many settings. I had a guide towards the end, a kid. The overriding theme in the dreams seemed to be one of overcoming unbeatable odds. I was fighting soldiers, cowboys, the Undead, (I used to constantly dream of battles with the Undead for most of my life), jungle tribes, shit—everybody. I kept winning the fights though. Eventually I became conscious. Take from that what you will Dream Analysts.

Once I could walk I was placed in the lockdown psych ward. How apropos. When I was a guard I also helped restrain many people in our lockdown psych ward. Also, the first person I ever helped restrain with a nurse was a Lithium OD victim. Life…full circles…yada, yada, yada.

I was very numb both mentally and physically. Except my feet. The bottoms of my feet were in fucking agony for almost two weeks. I could barely walk on them. I couldn't think long about anything and simple decisions were hard to make. I could barely speak coherently.

My actions were viewed as a suicide attempt. I was angrily informed of this by a nurse who interviewed me to see where my head was at. I tried to tell her that it was simply the most masochistic way I could think to punish myself and also the most dramatic way I could piss off my wife. I never said it was the *smartest* thing I could've chosen to do but then I was blind drunk at the time. I got mad about being in there but was released after a few days. I went home to finalize the destruction of my slice of the American Dream.

I sold my house, then returned the new truck to the dealer. I sold my gym on eBay at a disgusting loss. I fit in one more DWI, which put me at two in less than five years thereby making me a felon in New York. Then I sold the car.

My family moved in with me into my parents' small house and the whole situation collapsed rapidly from there. I wanted out of the whole mess so bad. I prayed for it. I had known before I ever got married that I was not ready for the responsibilities and challenges of raising kids. Shit. I was no good just as a person. How could I take care of anyone else? My prophecy proved correct. I couldn't take it anymore. My wife and kids left for a new life without me.

The weight lifted from me was enormous. I was so relieved. And then I started missing them. Horribly. Life's a kick.

Ken's note: Again, a whole lot of glazing over of details here. What my wife and I experienced as I crumbled, what my kids had to deal with, what my parents endured as they tried to help, was all too personal to go into detail about. The situation was extremely bad for all involved. Much was mishandled or handled poorly but it made none of us a bad person because of it.

I felt like an utter failure as a husband, father, and son at this point but it didn't change the fact that I needed to be alone. If I was to ever help my son and my wife and her kids, then I needed time and space to make it happen. If I was ever going to be the person I should be, a help to all I touch, then that freedom had to be in place. I promised her I'd still help. I promised my parents I'd be OK. I am keeping my promises. I'm making it happen.

SEND IN THE MARINES

I must backtrack just a tad here. Before my family left me, I'd already begun to see the futility in the medical approach. My life statistics were proving to me that I was not getting better no matter what the doctors tried to do for me. I could barely maintain myself each day let alone get better. I would have been happy to just feel LESS bad than I did but it was proving impossible to achieve even that for any length of time. So yes, I was fast losing faith in any doctor's ability to make me feel better.

Basically, I was fed up with my life. I was scared, depressed, and dissociative all the time. Any sense of my manliness had been taken from me. That in itself felt like rape. But instead of losing my innocence, I had lost my strength. I was no longer a Warrior. That sense of "no matter what, I'll power through this" no longer existed. I was a baby.

I was aware of the existing medications that applied to my illness and I was almost to the end of that list. There was almost nothing new left to try. Knowing this like I did was the same as being handed a death sentence. I was not going to get better. Worse—I was going to continue to devolve into a poorer and poorer quality of life. A life sure to be filled with psych ward visits and the prospect of never being truly happy or calm or sane ever again. A burden to my family forever and one day a ward of the State. That's how bad I felt and the logical conclusion I could see my life heading towards.

That's another fun-filled aspect to bipolar disorder. Your mind doesn't work right but it does in fact continue to work. You are painfully cognizant of where you're at and where you're headed. Sometimes I used to think it would be so much easier if I could just go full psychotic. Just head on into my fantasy world and let what may happen, happen. It was too much work to fight this monster and it seemed clear that a win wasn't possible anyhow, so why bother?

Somewhere in here the Marine in me resurfaced. He hadn't been around for a couple of years. He was fed up with the lack of results and he decided to reassert his presence. Marines don't fail. Period. This Marine decided to get proactive with his treatment. I wish I could say that I charged right into getting better but it wasn't so. A kernel of the fight I used to have in me began to poke its way up through the haze of my pain and weakness. Like the first flowering plant on the burned forest floor my hope took root.

THE BATTLE FOR GOOD HEALTH IS ENGAGED

KEN JENSEN

THE FEDERAL GOVERNMENT CONFIRMS THAT I AM, IN FACT, NUTS

The first thing that had to change for me was to rid my life of as much stress as possible. I had to cut out anything that was adding to or irritating my symptoms. For me, and this caused a whole other pile of problems, the first thing to go was work. I could not tolerate anything about holding down a job. This one thing was actually something I'd fought with for twenty years. I never could tolerate being an employee. I know many can't, but it seemed to be extra special bad for me.

So I stopped trying to work. That part wasn't hard. I used to get panic attacks or fall into a deep depression just pulling into the parking lot of any job I ever held. So the thought of never reporting to someplace ever again was a big relief.

But now I had money problems. My father actually pushed me into attempting to get disability. This was hard on my ego and I figured I wouldn't win a disability case. It is a gray area legally. How do you prove something as intangible as mental illness? I tried once on my own and it wasn't approved. I started again a year later but this time I got a lawyer. That seems to be the only way you can win.

I got things straightened out with my psych. I had reinstated myself with the same doc at the VA. He was a very big help in getting me approved. It wasn't too hard for him. I more than met the qualifications for someone barely able to function in society, let alone hold a job.

There is an evaluation criteria that doctors use to rate just how screwed up a person may be. The resulting number weighs heavily in a judge's decision on whether or not to award you and to what degree. I came in just under the wire for being unable to function properly in a social setting. According to this system I was incapable of leading a normal life. As if I needed that chart to tell me that. But it was nice to know of its existence.

It took me two years to complete the whole process to obtain disability and I've heard horror stories that took longer. But I didn't give up. That was a long haul issue. I still had immediate problems to take care of first.

ARE WE NOT SPEAKING THE SAME LANGUAGE HERE?

I was hit with a lot of legal problems due to my DWI. They made me jump through a lot of hoops. The first year was a nightmare to me. I am in no way denying I broke the law or downplaying the severity of this particular offense. I am thankful that I didn't hurt anyone, myself included. If I'd hurt another I know it would have been something that could have potentially wiped me out inside whether bipolar or not. But my illness made the whole process they put me through so much worse.

I was being punished as a drunk. Period. My illness was of no concern to anyone. So I had to make it a concern. But first I had to complete my community service. Day labor. I was so incredibly enraged while doing those days. At the same time my low back gave out. Bad. I worked hurt many days and avoided direct labor as much as possible without them punishing me by discounting the day but I was in a great deal of pain. This would later become part of my disability.

An MRI proved that I did indeed have a bunch of new damage that had developed inside the three years since my last MRI. Bulging disks, thin disks, tears, arthritis. I accomplished an incredible amount of damage down there without knowing it. I got through the labor punishment and then had to deal with the psychological punishment of group therapy to help me deal with my addiction issues.

I had a big, big problem with these groups. I knew what I was about. I was also very well read on the topic of addiction, and the military had crammed a lot of training about it down my throat. I had been to AA meetings off and on for years and I knew they spoke the truth at these sessions. I'm trying to say I wasn't in the dark about being an alcoholic. I was pretty clear on that. My life had amply proven to me that I shouldn't drink.

I had to endure three classes a week for about two and a half hours a day. They were causing me to lose my mind. Literally. They took place in the mornings and I was a night guy. So I went to each class pre-exhausted. Plus, with the depression I normally experienced, I just wanted to sleep. I wanted sleep so bad all the time.

I will say that my counselor, Dan, was very cool and he sincerely wanted to help me. Thankfully, I was able to convince these people that my main problem in life was from bipolar disorder. I'm sure you know by now that drinking and drugs proved disastrous for me over time. They ruined me. I knew this. But the reason I had taken up drinking again was to escape the noise in my head.

I used to describe the black energy in my mind as a mouse on crack running in circles inside my skull. I became capable of coherently focusing on ten separate thoughts in my mind, simultaneously. None of them had anything to do with each other and meant nothing. They were just there. Then my brain would try to follow each new line of thought extending from those first ten. It is an overwhelming amount of data to process and my head would just about burn up tracking it all and I could not make it stop trying.

So I was released from the program after three months. I was ecstatic because it was a mandatory one-year deal. Essentially, I had passed their class. I was not kicked out. I satisfied them and this in turn satisfied the legal people with whom I still had to work.

So I was free from direct punishment by the legal system. Mostly. I was still on probation but that's way better than the first two punishments. My home life still sucked. I am not going into detail here. Suffice to say I needed my wife and kids to go elsewhere. I needed that to happen in the worst way. And they did. That was the second to last great stressor in my life that I could do something about. But it was a hell of a thing to wish for.

The very last stressor was my mountain of new debt. When I won my disability case, most of that was paid off in one shot. Another humongous relief. I must stress here: I am NOT saying everyone should rush to quit their jobs and get rid of their spouses and/or kids. But for me it was a necessity. I still love both my ex-wives in my own way but none of us belonged together. And I would give my life for my son.

PLOP, PLOP, FIZZ, FIZZ, OH WHAT A RELIEF IT AIN'T

So the external issues were resolved the best they could be. That gave me room to deal with the internal issues. I have been a mechanic many times over the years. I have fixed all kinds of unrelated equipment. Everything is similar when it comes to troubleshooting. The body is no different. What should be happening but isn't and why? What is happening that shouldn't and why? That's where I started. I knew that the meds were doing no good and I'd read enough and seen enough while working in the hospital to know they were definitely doing me some harm. If nothing else, they were proving ineffective for me.

I also knew they didn't truly repair anything. They were a Band-Aid. They treated symptoms but really did nothing to resolve the actual problem. Now, for many years I didn't care. My head was so bad I'd have gladly eaten horseshit if you told me it would make me feel better. But no longer. I wanted improvement and I wanted to be proactive. Meds are reactive.

It's like when you have heartburn and eat Rolaids constantly. Sure, you feel better after eating the antacid but the burn comes back. If you learned what was really causing the burn and repaired it, you would no longer need the antacid. You have fixed the problem for real. The antacid was just another Band-Aid fixing nothing.

I used that metaphor specifically because I actually experienced it. I ate antacids for most of the three years before my big improvements in life. I kept jars at work, in my desk at home, in my backpack, and in my car. I had heartburn constantly. As I repaired my mind I experienced the convenient byproduct of no longer having heartburn. It simply dawned on me one day that I hadn't reached for a Rolaids in months. Holy shit! That was like a little unexpected gift from me to me.

KEN JENSEN

POISON? NO THANKS. I REALLY COULDN'T EAT ANOTHER BITE

I've often read that bipolar disorder is a condition we're born with. I believe it can be but I also think it can be manufactured. Either way you shouldn't settle into thinking you are powerless to do something about it. To do so ignores the larger picture of what else may be contributing. It's too much of a crutch.

You might think, "Oh well, it's genetic. I'm stuck with it and I'll have to deal with it the best I can." You're partly right. I mean, if it's in you, it's in you. But in the beginning of your illness showing its face you need to know that it's not your fault, especially if you've led a healthy life in comparison to mine.

Maybe you did do something to help it along as I did. Regardless, give yourself some room to feel okay with the fact that you're sick knowing that it's temporarily out of your hands.

It's not a matter of will power or "bucking up and taking it like a man." I am eternally stunned by the ignorance of the "healthy" telling very sick, very bipolar people to "snap out of it" or "it's all just in your head." They have absolutely no idea what they're saying and how unbelievably cruel it is to say to the sick person. But I digress.

The key thing here is you shouldn't lie down and just accept your fate. Do not believe you have no say in this and there is nothing to be done about it from your end. Because from there you are too eager to start taking medication and further assuming that is your only option for good health. It's NOT the only option and as far as I'm concerned, it's not even a good one.

Here's why I say that: look at the little you have read of my past (and believe me, you've only read a little). It is very easy to see how my bipolar disorder could have been helped along by all the mind-bending substances I willingly ingested over the years. Now consider the reverse: if street drugs are bad for you because they damage your body and negatively alter your perception of reality over time, what makes you think that the psychotropics are all that different in what they are doing to you? They are not a food. Your body doesn't need them to function. Also you are specifically taking them to alter your frame of mind, right? And too many people like me have proven through years of experience that they aren't really fixing anything. There's nothing to argue here. Just look at how my life panned out for the eight years I tried to do it the pharmaceutical way.

I realize many people have not had any experience with chemicals that matches mine, or at least not to the extent that I did. But in reflecting on the probable results of all my partying, it brings to light how the mind can be affected by substances that do not belong in the body.

The first of these are obvious. If you drink alcohol, smoke cigarettes/chew tobacco, or take any kind of illegal drugs you must stop. No religion out of me here or talks on legal matters. Just good health. Drinkin', smokin', and partyin' all have a massively negative effect on your state of mind if you are bipolar. You may think these things, whichever of them you may do, relax you. You're kidding yourself. All of these substances are irritants to your condition. And you are reinforcing the bad stuff that's going on inside your head if you are bipolar.

I have smoked cigarettes on and off for a few years and I chewed tobacco for maybe seven years in total. Always to relax. Much like the weed discussion with my first psych, I found out that our nicotine is deceptively stimulating. You may be aware of this in that you know that morning smoke is the best one. Sets your head for the day but it also is a pick-me-up right? Rhetorical question. It is. And the stimulant part is what hammers those of us in the bad nerves sector of society. Your smoke/chew is driving you nuts.

Forget the rest of the obvious health issues. Focus on the fact that your frazzled nerves are being caused in a large part by the thing you do to calm down. That should help you to quit in some fashion.

THE ENVIRONMENT ISN'T ENVIRONMENTALLY SOUND

Anything that does not belong in the body has an exponentially stronger negative effect on our little group. Now, think about how polluted the world has become. Seems like there's now a reason why every other food is no longer safe to eat. It's pretty much a cliché in our world at this point. But it's also a scary fact. There really are many things in our food, water, and air that can contribute to having bipolar disorder.

The list is staggering: **mercury** in our fish, an endless amount of varied **toxins** in our drinking **water, hormones** and **antibiotics** designed for animals in our **meat and milk.**

The very **air** we breathe indoors being many times more polluted than outdoor air.

The **hydrogenation** present in fried foods, crackers, and cookies. (You may as well be eating battery acid in comparison to what those extra hydrogen molecules are doing to your insides.)

The **medicines** some of us take. (This is a whole book in itself on the harms caused by pharmaceuticals.)

The **medicines** we take to **counteract** the side effects of OTHER medicines we take.

The insane amounts of **pesticides** floating freely in our food supply.

The **high fat** and **empty carbohydrate** meals so many seem to prefer.

The **aspartame** and all other **artificial sweeteners** in our diet sodas and other foods (want your panic attacks to abate? Stop ingesting ANY artificial sweeteners.)

The high amounts of **caffeine** many of us enjoy, and so on.

Not that very long ago most of this simply did not exist. We are cursed via our own technology. All of these things can affect your bipolar disorder. Much of it may even be the CAUSE of it or at the very least is contributing to its continual assault on your sanity. If you want to feel better then you must begin to take great care in watching what you throw down the hatch. Those of us who are bipolar are extra sensitive to the nasty crap out there.

Your body is very resilient and will try to offset any harm you cause it, but it has a limit. One day it will rebel. And you don't have to be blatantly abusing yourself as I did for the rebellion to take place. But this is common sense. Doesn't it stand to reason that if you treat your body the best you can it should have some sort of positive effect on your mental health? Sure it does! It's step one to getting better.

THE ICE IS THIN BUT YOU CAN CROSS THIS LAKE

Now I also knew that stopping my meds would be bad. **DO NOT STOP YOUR MEDS BEFORE TALKING TO YOUR DOCTOR!!!** I kept taking mine while I searched for a better treatment plan. When I found what I believed to be a reputable system I weaned off of my meds. I did so in a planned, incremental, safe fashion.

For those of you who've been on meds for any length of time, you'll probably remember how long it took for them to bring you any kind of relief (if you were fortunate enough to get that far). Due to their action in the body it can take even longer to safely get off them than it did to build up to the maintenance level you're at now.

You have to be incredibly careful when you begin to taper off. Depending on the types and amounts of meds you're on, it could take months to safely stop. If you come off of meds too fast you could crash. You could go into withdrawal same as when you stop smoking, drinking, or drugging. But unlike hardcore drugs, the legal meds can jack you up worse when they run out. Not everybody. Don't worry. I'm just overstating this rather than risking the problems you could develop if I hadn't made it clear.

When it comes time to consider stopping your meds, you will need to clear it with your doctor. The company I am going to tell you about will develop a plan to get you through this phase and onto their products. But your doctor has to know what you're doing. If you pursue disability as I did, then everything about your treatment must be documented.

If you go this route, your new plan is going to be nutrient based. You are going to be giving your body the raw materials it needs to combat your bipolar disorder. Explain this to your doctor and get him on board. If he balks, then find a doctor who is willing to help you with a holistic approach.

On a side note and this is totally up to you, you may want to stay on your meds and have it documented as such while you are going through any disability case proceedings. It is hard enough to get your doctor to agree to your taking a holistic approach to your health. I feel confident most judges would be even LESS understanding and view your actions as one who won't play by the rules. The judge wants to see compliance with all medically accepted attempts to heal you or maintain you. Keep this in mind if you decide it is necessary to pursue a disability case.

If you are fine with holding a job and just need your head to settle then forget disability and get on my program immediately. You'll be back at work in no time!

IT'S THE LITTLE THINGS THAT COUNT

At one point earlier in my search for help I went to a nutritionist. At the time I was lifting hard in the gym and I ate bodybuilder clean. After a few hours with this lady it turned out that I was missing nothing in my diet. I was eating in a much healthier fashion than most and I ate a lot more food by volume than an inactive person. But I was still whacked.

My take on this is not that I was wrong in my approach to nutrition. It was that I still needed more nutrients than what I could get from my food. It would seem that many people can get by with less of these materials in their bodies or maybe folks like us have a greater need for them than non-afflicted people. Either way, you need way more than you'll ever get from your food no matter how well or how much you eat.

This is a very important thing I discovered from lifting weights and constantly striving to become bigger and stronger. The longer we lift the harder it is to keep making gains so we are more willing to try various substances to keep progressing. I am only referring to nutritional supplements here.

Bodybuilders don't have any doubts about the veracity of nutrition and what the body needs to function at an optimal level. We are actually more concerned with operating at a much higher level than what is normal to most. Due to this mindset we are more willing to experiment with foods and supplements without needing to see scientific proof in the form of studies and such.

Oh, it helps us to decide what route to take if there actually is data to prove the veracity of a product, but we'll go ahead and consume it regardless if we think it might help us gain one more inch on our arms or bump up our numbers in pounds moved in any lift. We don't care. If we think it might work we try it. This then leads to proof gained from stats. If we get bigger or stronger, then it must be working. If not, then it's probably crap or at least the brand itself is. That was the mindset I had when I began taking the product I'm about to share with you.

This very topic is a never-ending source of painful amusement to me. There is no end to reports on the news of "discoveries" in the health field of better ways to eat for good health or magical substances that someone with a title "discovered" that will benefit your mind or body. I haven't seen one yet that hasn't already been something that athletes of all types have known to be fact for decades before the good doctor's report became known.

For that matter you can also look to the East for proof of the benefits gained by eating various herbs and nutrients of all sorts. Those folks have 3,000 years of proof consisting of relief from many ailments and the lack of instances of these ailments in their societies to begin with.

I tell you all of this to prove a point. I was highly receptive to experimenting with any logical means of supplementation if there was enough existing data or "buzz" showing that others were getting good results. I didn't need a doctor to verify the results if others were saying something simply worked. This perspective led me to my first and most profound breakthrough in finding relief from my symptoms.

AND THEN, GOD SMILED UPON ME

I found **Truehope** quite by accident. There was an article in Discover Magazine back in 2005. It was about mental health and nutrition's possible role in maintaining it. It was also about a Canadian company that developed a vitamin and mineral mix that successfully treated depression and bipolar disorder. That caught my eye!

The company started with two friends. Dave was a pig farmer who found that when his animals became overly aggressive, he could calm them with the right mix of vitamins and minerals. Tony was a friend whose family was shattered by the effects of bipolar disorder. His wife's father committed suicide and later she did as well. She was bipolar. His daughter was bipolar and became psychotic because of it. She was seemingly beyond help. Then his son became angry and aggressive and was diagnosed as bipolar.

To Dave, this seemed similar to how the pigs sometimes behaved. So the two put their heads together and came up with a human version of the mix. They gave it to Tony's son and his symptoms disappeared. His daughter was given the mix and her symptoms soon dissipated too. She was supposedly incurable. She became fine and went on to raise a family of her own, not to mention, becoming a staunch advocate of her father's company and this way of fighting the disease. She went from a statistically lost soul to healthy fighter for the mentally ill.

This story impacted me. I ordered some product and began taking it. Within weeks, at one of the worst times of my life, I began to feel relief. I was still a mess but I definitely felt better. My head was clearer and my panic attacks backed way down.

But after a handful of months I completely ran out of money and had to go back on my meds. Something was better than nothing. I got worse again. Nine months later I was able to get back on the products and I became markedly better. Combined with the settling of most major issues in my life, I got better even faster this time around.

Go to http://www.truehope.com and register on the site. Don't worry, it's free and allows you access to the all the massive amounts of information within and helps the staff to assist you in the best way possible.

EMPowerPlus is their flagship product and you need it in you. It provides the vitamins and minerals your mind desperately needs in the amounts required to combat your illness. We need more nutrients than the normal person to function properly. And we need them in the <u>proper ratios</u> to be effective. That is a key difference to be aware of. We're special that way.

The high amounts of certain nutrients may seem too much or cause you to think they'd be toxic. This is a direct result of the training you've received from the media and/or government who don't know better or don't want you to know better. If you don't believe me, then I ask that you remember I got better as soon as I began taking these supplements. There are more reasons to trust me and Truehope than just this one, but let's keep the painfully obvious in the forefront of this discussion. Whatever you may think if you disagree with me...I got better. If you want to get better, then do what I do. Can we all agree that that makes sense?

The amounts of nutrients suggested as optimal by the FDA are ludicrous! Even for totally healthy people. I could really tear into a rant here but that's a little off topic for right now. Just trust me when I say the FDA does NOT have your best interests at heart.

As I learned from my visit with the nutritionist so long ago, eating well just won't cover it. We require an inordinate amount of nutrients to keep our disease at bay. But it can be controlled. That is what Truehope is all about.

They offer a few other key nutrients that help for specific conditions. For example: my highs and lows had been stabilized for many months but minor panic attacks began creeping back into my life; nothing devastating but enough to cause me concern and a small amount of worry. I called Truehope. (You should know that you may call them and speak at any length about your problems and it is free. No charge.) They had me begin taking large amounts of **inositol** and **choline**. They carry someone else's brand for these two items.

I was told to get some in me right away and not to wait for their batches in the mail. They told me to go to a health food store and buy someone else's product for the moment. The counselor told me I would feel better right away. She was right! I calmed down within two days. The panic tapered way off and then was no more.

You can call their help desk right now as long as it's during office hours. You don't have to be a member or a customer. The people are phenomenally friendly and are driven to help you experience relief from your symptoms. They will never try to hard sell you anything.

If you have some non-bipolar/depression issue that the counselor happens to be familiar with, you'll find they can offer help there, too. Not always but if they know something, they'll share. They'll point you toward a resource that may help even if it's outside of Truehope. They are fantastic folks!

Understand one thing: Truehope does not claim to be a cure. But you may experience so much relief that it seems like they are. It's entirely possible that your symptoms may vanish. They will walk you through everything you must do in regards to your meds and properly utilizing their products.

They will even speak to your doctor for you to help him/her understand why they should have faith in the Truehope nutrients.

Just like how it used to be with your meds, you will have to take **EMPowerPlus** forever to stay okay. But unlike meds, you will be consuming things that actually belong in your body.

Once you reach www.truehope.com you will see links at the bottom of the page. As you click on a link, a dropdown menu will actually rise up providing specific information broken down into segments pertaining to that one link.

Take your time and slowly browse each one and you will find most, if not all of your questions, will get answered without even entering the site.

I want to make this abundantly clear: Truehope is the number one single best thing I ever did to fight my bipolar disorder. *I have just handed you a gift of enormous importance if you suffer from bipolar disorder or severe depression. Do not dismiss my gift. You would do so at your own peril. It's that serious and that effective. Out of everything I suggest you do to feel better, this is the one that is most important.*

If your money is limited or if other steps I show you are too tough or inconvenient for you right now, that's fine. If anyone understands all that it's me. But do everything in your power to get on Truehope's products. Do what the counselors tell you to do. Stick to the plan they develop for you. Be honest with the info they ask of you. They'll need to know everything in order to help you. And they really do want to help you. You'll thank me for this one day.

OH BUT IT'S SO GOOD FOR YOU!

If your body's not healthy then there is no way you can realistically hope for your mind to be. They are connected and dependant on each other. Your next step is to improve your eating habits. You should already be taking **EMPowerPlus,** which will cover all your vitamin and mineral needs.

There are a few other nutrients you may end up taking via Truehope like choline and inositol. I take both of them to prevent panic attacks and they work. **EMPowerPlus** will also cover your vitamin and mineral needs in the gym. There is so much to be said about proper diet. There is even more to be said for what we bipolars need to take in to heal. The following is <u>general</u> good eating practices and specific substances bipolar folks need to get into their day.

Eat fish once in awhile. Yeah, yeah—mercury content. I know. But once or twice a week should be fine.

Eat chicken but stick to white meat—breasts. No legs or thighs. Grill or broil. This lets any fat present drip down and away from your meat rather than soak in it as when frying.

Buy lean cuts of beef. No marbling.

Oatmeal is great but make sure it's whole oats. Once they grind down the oats for the faster cooking version you start to lose the benefits.

Eat vegetables as much as possible. But they must be fresh or at least frozen. Canned vegetables are no good. They're devoid of most of the good stuff you're trying to get into your diet due to the packaging process. When it comes to veggies I have a few simple rules: the darker green they are the better. The chlorophyll that makes plants green is packed with good stuff.

Now here's a broader rule to use when building a **salad.** When choosing your **veggies** get **one of every color.** I'm serious. Different colors correspond to different nutrients. Choose many colors and you end up taking care of your fiber, phytonutrient, trace mineral and other micronutrient needs. Plus you will find that the resulting flavor mix is so tasty that you will forego the dressing. It would be overkill. Make a nice pretty salad and you won't need will power to avoid the condiments.

Fruit. Eat it in its whole form. Just like it is when the farmer picked it. Your goal here is to avoid processed foods. Eat an apple, not applesauce. Eat grapes. Don't drink grape juice. Once food is processed it either has additives that are no good for you or the processing destroys the nutrients within. You lose out either way.

Drink lots of water. At least the recommended eight glasses a day. A whole lot more if you are exercising. It flushes you out. Helps remove toxins from your system. Keep this in your mind. Your body is mostly water by far. Water is the transport source for everything that takes place in your body. If you were stranded in the wilderness, you could literally live for months with very little to no food. But you'd only last a few days without water.

You must **avoid dehydration** and it can sneak up on you insidiously. Sometimes the fatigue or lethargy you feel is only there because you're thirsty but don't recognize it as such. You don't have to be laboring hard for this to happen.

Dehydration can also masquerade as hunger. By reaching for a snack you're only making it worse. Drinking water keeps you feeling full to some degree and you will snack less. This will keep you feeling better and help you avoid unwanted pounds.

You will not retain water if you drink a lot of it. If you are taking in water all the time, your body will note this fact and feel comfortable with ridding the extra. It knows that more is coming so it will not tell itself to store any. It's important to stay hydrated. If you fall even a hair below optimal water levels in your system, your brain will start malfunctioning. It's part of the reason why hangovers are so painful. Your body has used up so much water to flush out the alcohol that your brain is deflating.

Your brain has even more water in it percentage-wise than the rest of your body. Run low on water and your brain literally starts to sink into itself causing pain. I realize that is an extreme example but I threw it in there to make the point clear. We bipolar folks are way more susceptible to anything messing with the delicate balance of things in our minds. No need to exacerbate the situation by drinking too little water.

Protein. Specifically **whey protein isolate.** Another double whammy of goodness. This type of protein is the best for growth when lifting weights so I've been eating it for years anyway. But for those of us who've also been on meds for any length of time, it has another benefit.

The meds we take for our illness build up like any other toxin in our bodies. They seem to get stored in our muscle tissue as they easily bond to any proteins. Like I said earlier, they're not a food. They serve no functional purpose in our bodies. We don't metabolize them. They do their job and then are excreted. Except not 100%. Some residue is left behind. Over the years this residue begins to cause more problems for us. As it breaks free from its storage site we become, in essence, overmedicated. Even if we've discontinued our meds, the residue continues to harm us over time with its sporadic presence. It has to go.

The whey protein isolate will bond to any meds present in your bloodstream, thereby creating a particle that is too large to pass into your brain, or anywhere else, and your body will then excrete it.

You have the side benefit, if that's how you want to view it, of having a small, healthy snack in the form of a protein shake. It counts as a meal. Great for folks who want to shave a little excess from their diet plan and still get proper nutrition.

Glutamine. This stuff is like manna from heaven to every system of your body. Again, I have eaten it for years because it is a massive aid in healing from physical labor. It is incredibly good for your immune system and it has a direct effect on bipolar symptoms. If you're lacking it, you will feel worse.

Glutamine is just an amino acid. It's in most of the food you eat anyway, particularly meat. It's one of the few nutrients you can still get a lot of from your food. But we need all the help we can to feel better compared to level-headed folks. So take a little extra each day. I use a micronized (broken down to a very tiny size) version to ensure the best absorption.

Omega 3. Fish oil basically. If you want a healthy head you MUST take this stuff. It is also highly beneficial to your heart, hormone production, your vision, lowered triglycerides, your joints, and it even aids in fat burning. It's a great anti-inflammatory as well. But key for us is its mood-stabilizing properties and its ability to alleviate depression. Keeps you calm and pulls you up out of the hole if you're swinging that way. Take it regularly and you won't have to be retrieved in either direction. Avoid them both in the first place.

Omega 3 is crucial to the health of your myelin sheath (the protective coat wrapped around your nerves). It may also help in the production of more dendrites (the little arms connected to the ends of each nerve cell that allow the cells to talk to each other—more dendrites, more communication potential).

There is one brand I swear by. Go to http://www.omegabrite.com. I have many reasons why I prefer their brand above all others. Here they are: Omegabrite is 90% omega 3, which is three times more potent than most brands. Omega 3 **in fish oil** is made up of **EPA** and **DHA**. These are the **essential fatty acids** you may have heard of. They are essential because our bodies cannot produce them; we have to get them from our food.

Omegabrite's version is 70% EPA, the highest concentration available. EPA is a natural anti-inflammatory molecule. So that's a 7:1 ratio of EPA to DHA. The high amount of EPA is important for the following reason. We can hold on to DHA but the more crucial EPA is used up rapidly to counteract the inflammatory omega 6's that are so prevalent in our diet. Our omega 3's should be present in equal amounts to omega 6's—1:1 ratio for optimal health. But our modern diet completely goes the wrong way. It is more like 20:1 in favor of the omega 6's! That is totally backwards for good health. This causes an overall inflammatory response in our bodies leading to cardiac disease, *depression*, asthma, arthritis and so on. So it is important to go heavy on the omega 3's and heavy again on the EPA. Omegabrite kills two birds with one stone.

Flaxseed has omega 3's and 6's too, but no EPA or DHA. There is nothing wrong with flaxseed. It is really good stuff in its own right. But when combating my bipolar disorder, I want the best.

GARBAGE IN—GARBAGE OUT. EXACTLY WHAT ARE YOU TRYING TO PROVE?

Hoo-boy! In all honesty? It's easier to just keep in mind what you should eat. The list is shorter. But let's have a go at it. No particular order here:

Fat. Has to go. I am referring to saturated fats. Some fats like in olive oil are actually very good for you and fats play an important part in hormone production and nervous system communication. No butter but if you must, eat butter rather than margarine. Margarine is trans-fatty acid city. I also look at it this way—butter is a natural product, margarine is combined oil and water. To my way of thinking—yuck! So go with butter but limit it as much as possible.

Trim all visible fat from your meats. Easy enough right? Don't want it on you? Then don't put it in you.

No deep-frying—ever! Frying of that type is like defending why you smoke cigarettes. Not a winnable argument. Period. Deep frying adds oils to your food and the process turns the fat into carcinogenic (cancer causing) crud or transforms the oil into trans-fatty acids. TFAs are in French fries by default. Skip the fries.

Trans-fatty acids are bad because they act in a similar way as do free radicals. They are a naturally unstable molecule and will attach themselves to parts of your body in an attempt to chemically stabilize themselves. This wreaks havoc with your health.

They are common in fried foods and many baked goods. They are added to chips and cookies and pastries to make them crisp and fluffy and to extend the shelf lives of these products.

They make fats more stable at room temperature, allowing them to keep from going rancid. They make your food taste better too by affecting texture. But they are just about the worst things you could ever ingest. Avoid buying them directly and avoid creating them by frying your foods.

Breading, as on fish. Nope.

Soda (Colas in specific). The phosphoric acid present in both regular and diet sodas wipes out valuable minerals from your body as it attempts to neutralize it. The sugar in any regular soda is terrible in too many ways to list here. The artificial sweeteners are even more dangerous than the sugar. That leads to the following:

Aspartame. Causes panic attacks and generally screws with your head, among other things. Nasty stuff. Other sugar-free sweeteners aren't any better. If you have to choose, you might as well stick with the sugar. At least it's natural, something your body understands. This leads to:

Sugar. There is a plethora of info out there showing how excessive sugar causes truckloads of problems for us. Way, way, way too many to list here. So look at it this way: it makes you fat, makes your mood go up and down, makes you tired, and pushes you into diabetes. That's enough reasons right there to avoid it.

Beware fat-free foods. Companies will jack up the sugar content to make up for the lack of taste created by removing the fat. You get fat anyway because of the empty calories they put in the fat's place. Double whammy there.

Condiments: Mayo is mostly fat, butter is pure fat, ketchup has a lot of sugar, jelly is pure sugar, gravy is usually all fat, and diet gravy is too nasty to consider. Dressing is usually full of fat. Light dressing is good but watch for sugar content. Fat-free mayo? I guess if you're feeling brave. But since it's a manufactured product I'd just as soon go with regular mayo. Soy sauce has an incredible amount of salt. Use sparingly.

Processed flour. Flour does not look white. They make it that way. And once they have, it is no longer much of a food source. It's just fluffy sugar. Literally.

Ice cream. A big no-no. Sugar, fat, emulsifiers, and who knows what else. You're gettin' attacked on multiple fronts when you eat ice cream.

Peanut butter and jelly on white bread. You should only eat this when scooping lard from a bucket with a spoon is just too darned inconvenient.

Cold breakfast cereals. Same as white bread. They are processed right down to being pure sugars themselves. They started out as grains just like the bread. I don't care what health benefits they put on the label. They're lying for the most part.

Cream of Wheat. Same as white bread.

Egg yolks. They are not as bad as we've been led to believe, but they are high in fat, so eat sparingly. You'll find that if you put two whole eggs in with four or six egg whites and mix them, they taste fine when cooked. The protein in the yolks compliments the protein in the whites, as they are not the same. So a couple won't hurt.

Whole milk, 2% or 1%. Too much fat. Liquid butter in fact. The percentages are a marketing trick. Trust me. Go with skim. Interesting side note: There are many who believe ANY milk is no good, cow's milk that is, due to hormones, antibiotics, and the fact that cow's milk is for cows and not humans. I agree but I can't quit milk just yet. But I only drink skim.

Alcohol. When I first quit drinking as I left the Marines, I lost 25 pounds in the first week. The only thing I changed in my world was to stop drinking. 25 pounds!

Beer and booze is mostly sugar but for us, it's a mood-altering substance. Has to go. If you want relief from your bipolar disorder, you have to stop drinking. I also found that the hangovers would cause me to have panic attacks the next day. It may give you temporary relief from your symptoms but you're losing more than you're gaining.

Tobacco of any sort. I'll ignore the obvious bad health issues here and address our unique situation. Nicotine may relax you but it is a very strong stimulant. If you're manic or panicky, you're plenty stimulated already. Have to stop smoking.

St. John's Wort. This is a mistake. Due to different manufacturer's processing habits, who knows what you're really getting? Same with any herb actually, but this stuff directly acts on your mind. It's also been found that the Wort can cause those of us with bipolar to yo-yo. The calm you are seeking by ingesting it is not sustainable. It has the potential to bring on psychosis as well. We've got enough issues on our plates in my opinion. No need to add to it by messing with that delicate balance we're trying to maintain in our minds.

Coffee: It's a stimulant and I had a long period when I couldn't tolerate it myself. Made me nervous and panicky. I'm okay with it now but I only have a cup or two across the day. If you're having a hard time relaxing you may want to switch to teas. Drinking decaf in some way feels like a mortal sin to me but if you must, then go ahead. At least you won't be trouncing your nerves with the caffeine.

Energy drinks: white willow, guarana, caffeine, kola nut, etc. Red Bull might be creating havoc with your nerves. Those kinds of drinks are just stronger cups of coffee really. And most of them are packed with sugar and/or artificial sweeteners as well. If your nerves are shot and you want to stay lean, then you'd better skip them.

WOULD YOU PLEASE STOP EATING THAT? I'M SERIOUS! STOP EATING THAT!

You may be wondering why I laid out so much fat loss type info. "Why should I have to worry about that? I'm not fat. I'm stressed out," or something to that effect. It's simple really. Your brain needs all the help it can get to run right. It's part of the overall machine in respect to health. And it's already probably quite busy with trying to make itself feel better. I'm sure that's an issue you have it chewing on frequently throughout each and every waking moment of your life. So why add to its workload by bogging it down in sludge? Or causing it more work by forcing it to deal with bodily functions that are not up to par?

In order for your brain to fix itself, it needs to be free from unnecessary constraints. If your body is running smooth, then your mind is free to focus on itself.

You might not consciously feel anything wrong. But if you're putting junk into yourself, believe me, your subconscious mind knows. I'm not talking metaphysical or spiritual here. I mean physically. It's slowing down, getting cluttered. It's trying to keep up with all its chores as floor boss for the unit plus deal with the mess of misfiring neurons and helter skelter hormonal bursts or lack thereof. It needs nutrients, but is not getting them because you aren't putting them in.

Or you're losing nutrients as your body uses them up, neutralizing the crap you're eating that does more harm than good. Eating the wrong foods will cause both of those things to happen. Taking in anything toxic will cause it all to happen even faster. So you have no choice. You must take care of the machine as best as possible.

Now, do I stick to those lists I laid out like a saint? No. Not at all times. But pretty much! I have to. If you are in the hell I was or anywhere near it, wouldn't you want to do every single last thing in your power that you could to make it stop? Me too. Help your body help your head.

WHAT IN THE WIDE, WIDE WORLD OF SPORTS IS GOING ON IN THERE?

Heavy metals in your system can be the cause of your symptoms. Bad bacteria anywhere within you can cause all kinds of things to go wrong.

You may have Candida, a yeast infection that goes incorrectly diagnosed many times and is a cause of our symptoms.

If the good bacteria in your digestive tract have been wiped out by antibiotics or because of some other reason you must replace them. http://www.truehope.com has a probiotic formula to replace them.

See, without the proper bacteria present in your intestines, you can't even digest the nutrients you take in to feel better. You can be eating perfectly, but if it's not being absorbed, what's the difference? Might as well be eating dirt for all the good it's doing you. This can cause all sorts of painful abdominal problems; diarrhea, irritable bowel syndrome, you name it.

The problems you develop elsewhere in the body from not being able to absorb nutrients is far more extensive yet. Any of that can cause a cornucopia of pain anywhere in your body.

You may have Lyme's Disease and not know it. It can be incorrectly diagnosed as something else, then you improperly medicate and now you have two major problems on your hands. And you're in pain. It's been found that Lyme's can play a huge part in developing bipolar disorder.

The list of relatively unknown causes for our symptoms is extensive. The best book I've ever found that addresses all of it is called "**Too Good to Be True? Nutrients Quiet the Unquiet Brain**" by **David Moyer**. This man opened my eyes WAY up to the potential causes of our illness. He also goes heavily into how the medical community is failing us. He knows from personal experience as a family member AND as a professional.

My close family was amazed at how many things he had to say that matched what I either knew or instinctively felt. It's not just my opinion that this gentleman is spot on. It's one of the best books I've ever read on the topic, and his experiences and opinions match most of mine.

"TAKE THE PAIN!" YEAH, WELL, NOT IF YOU DON'T HAVE TO

When you're in pain, your mind is further burdened. It simply makes everything else in your life worse. If you hurt, your mood will worsen. If your mood worsens, any pain you have can intensify. The two feed each other. You have to try to eliminate all the pain you can. Try to figure out why you're hurting beyond anything blatantly obvious. You may be limited here. Maybe something catastrophic has happened to you physically. But you may be adding to it unawares. You can get used to pain.

This is a widespread area. There are many reasons why someone could be hurting. I will share the things I've learned. Pain is simply signals in your mind at its most basic. That's it. That is why hypnotized people or people who get hurt a lot during their workday can tolerate more of it. They control how their mind handles those signals. They can turn it off or consciously handle more than others. It's really all in your head. I'm talking purely of the pain signals.

Don't misunderstand me. I know many people go to a doctor, in agony for whatever reason, and if unable to find a physical cause the doctor then says, "It's all in your head." That is NOT what I am saying here. As far as that goes, many of us have probably been told the same thing about our mental symptoms. What I'm getting at here is that once any clear-cut reasons are eliminated and you can't figure out why you hurt, it may be because something is acting on your mind or acting on a part of your body and causing a real pain.

Stress stored in your mind and body both can cause pain. You're harboring a negativity about something, probably many somethings and it is causing actual pain. That is another whole book topic right there. For now, believe me when I tell you "your body stores negative energy from situations your mind could not handle, as stress and muscle tension in other areas of itself."

Try and picture the person in upper management who always solves the big problems at your job but forces everyone else to walk on eggshells in their presence. That's one type of the bottled stress, of which I speak.

The other main type of stress is more of a purely structural nature. Tab "A" is not lining up properly with slot "B." But it's not something you can easily locate and rid yourself of. You need to address your entire health scenario to get some of these other ethereal issues solved. That may sound a bit "New Age" to you, but I assure you it is not. Even these things boil down to body mechanics and better maintenance.

I'm not asking you to believe in some far-out trippy guru stuff. I'm just asking you to consider becoming a better owner/operator of your own machine.

Some of any pain you may have can be attributed to not directly caring for the various systems in your body. By following all the steps I cover for getting better, you will find that much of your physical pain goes away. That's part of the beauty of this systemic approach I discovered for relieving bipolar symptoms. Your body will rid itself of many other problems in the process. Like my heartburn. It just vanished after torturing me for three solid years. I was not trying to address that problem. Ever. But one day I realized it had been a long, long time since I'd needed an antacid. And that moment came a long time ago itself!

WE NEED TO TALK

This is critical. There is one area (at least regarding bipolar), in which I do agree with psychiatrists, psychologists, and therapists. That area is the need to talk it out. Talk therapy.

Call it whatever you'd like but you can't hold all your crap inside. It will definitely turn into a physical problem. Your physical health will suffer in some way that a doctor could easily put a name to.

But your mental health will surely crumble. You will destroy yourself by holding in your bad feelings, scary thoughts, questions, fears, ideas, assumptions, perspectives, etc. You need to release what's up in that noggin of yours.

It didn't amount to much at all, but whenever I was waiting to see a doctor or visiting one because I was in crisis, which meant panic, I immediately felt better just by being in their presence. And I felt demonstrably better the more I talked. Talking was good.

Ultimately, I could see how it wasn't achieving anything, except for the minor relief I got right then and there. I considered that an unuseful amount of help.

Now, to be fair, I can also see how a few of these people told me things I seriously needed to address and change about myself. They were dead on correct but I was in no place mentally to act on what they were saying. They were right but I was crippled.

This is one of the glitches with talk therapy. It is highly beneficial but fairly useless all by itself. It goes back to what I mean when I say you must address all areas of your life. Talk therapy is just one more tool, but an important one.

This is where my saint of a mother comes into the story. My whole life, I'd always talked to her far more than my father. She knew me best, second only to my wives. But, because she was my mother, she was willing to sit with me on the porch as I talked out every single little thing that was on my mind, day after day after day for months. This became part of my healing. It was not recognized as such, by her or me, until much later.

I shared everything with my mom that was tormenting me. Sometimes too much. Being my only close friend during my sickest years, she got to hear a few things from a son that a mother shouldn't hear. The incredible loneliness I was enduring made me crave female companionship even more than what could be considered normal. Poor Ma got to hear some details about this that I doubt she was glad to know.

But her willingness to just *listen* was golden! I needed that! I found many of my answers, answers that you are now benefitting from, by just rambling endlessly to the World's Most Patient Mother.

She usually didn't know what to say back to me but she tried to encapsulate what she thought I'd just told her. Or sometimes she'd just say the most encouraging and positive thing she could think of to try and boost my spirits.

This process allowed me to empty my mind of all within it, and lay it out clearly on the ground at my feet. I was able to examine myself via these conversations. As I became healthier from all my other steps, the talk sessions got clearer and deeper topics were made known to me, by me. I was able to drill down deeper into what was bothering me and why I thought that might be.

I gave my illness a coherent voice. It was almost like I was channeling it. I could hear how the illness would sound to a sane person by virtue of hammering it all out, endlessly, in conversation. I came to many, many smart conclusions as to how one can heal, by having these talks with my mom.

So, you need to find your version of "Mom" and get it all out of you. You also have the benefit of healing faster by doing the steps I offer in this book and you will reach your own healthier conclusions much, much faster than I ever did.

TALK!

WHEN THE BACK GOES, HAPPINESS CAN'T BE FAR BEHIND

Most of my pain centers in my damaged spine. Since I feel that is a common enough ailment for many of us, I'll share what I do to repair it the best I can.

You might need a new mattress. Maybe your pillow sucks more than you realize. Maybe you're lying around too much due to depression. That was a big one for me. If you sit in a chair all day at home or work, your chair might be killing you. You may be used to how you sit, not realizing you need the arms to be higher or the backrest is not supporting you well. Many people don't realize that structurally, the most pressure is on your spine when you are seated. Get up and move as much as possible during the day.

If your shoes are worn out, that will definitely show up in your back. As the soles become uneven, the load on your legs is different. One side of your body is now out of balance with the other. Get some new shoes.

Don't carry your wallet in your back pocket. Put it in the front. That fraction of an inch or so that one butt cheek sits higher than the other adds up over the years. Think about how braces work on a teenager's teeth. Get my point? It may not seem like much but an uneven load is an uneven load. One of my first chiropractors taught me that, years ago.

Tension in all the rear muscles of your body can keep you in back pain, neck pain and headaches. You need to stretch your calves, your hamstrings, your glutes, and even your thighs.

Find something upright. A pole or something like it is best. While wearing shoes and using one foot at a time, put your toes up against the pole, and place your heel as close as you can to the base of the pole. Now **slowly** pull yourself forward and try to bring your knee into the pole while keeping your leg straight. Go very slow and steady. If this is new to you, then you will only get so far. Hold the stretch for 20 or 30 seconds. Over time you will be able to stretch for a couple minutes and your knee will actually touch the pole.

Place your feet close together and bend down trying to touch the floor with your hands. Bend your knees as little as possible. Get as close as you can to the floor WITHOUT bending your back. Focus on keeping your chest upright. If you're still a foot away, don't worry. Hold the stretch for 30 seconds. Don't bounce, just hold. NEVER bounce when stretching.

Each day try to get a little closer. Eventually you will be able to touch the floor. Then start to try and get your knees to stay straighter. Once you've achieved that, try to palm the floor. You'll get there eventually. It may take weeks or even months but as you gain flexibility there will be less tension on your back. I like to palm the floor and hold it for two minutes. Your back will thank you.

If your back still hurts, find a good chiropractor. There is nothing to "believe in" here. Once again, it's just simple mechanics. Your nerves that allow you to feel everything and anything there is to feel, both good and bad, run through your spine. If the bones in your spine are not lined up on top of each other correctly, your nerves will be adversely affected. Your gall bladder could get a headache because a nerve in your back is being pinched. You can feel sick to your stomach because your back is messed up. Or some damn thing will just hurt somewhere.

Your entire messaging system from all your body parts to your brain runs through your spine. Doesn't it make sense to keep your spine nice and straight? Good and relaxed? Rhetorical question.

But chiropractors are like anything else. Find one you like and actually does you good. I've been to many. They're all similar but you really know it when you get a bad one or a guy has a technique that does not agree with you. Be patient. Go with your gut. Find a doctor who gets the job done and who comforts you with his words and knowledge. And remember, if your back has been hurting for a long time, then be patient as you work towards straightening it out. It's going to take some time to undo what you did.

I recently discovered this chiropractor's site:
http://chiropracticfamilyfitness.com
and added all his stretches and core strengthening exercises to my daily routine. **Dr. Larry's** routine is specifically for the spine. It differs from stretching the large muscle groups as I outlined above. Watch Dr. Larry's free video and combine his stretches with mine. I prefer to do his first then mine.

One last item: If your feet are messed up, everything above them most assuredly will be as well. If you're happy with your shoes, sneakers, or boots then the next step is to invest in a great pair of insoles. Go to
http://www.superfeet.com
and investigate. I use their stuff and the difference from other brands is astounding!

If your feet are really messed up as mine recently turned out to be, you should look into talking with a good podiatrist. Get some custom orthotics made for you. While writing this book I had that done for me. Heaven! Unbelievable how good my feet feel now!

Make your feet happy and the rest of your body will thank you. Make your body happy and you will BE happy!

BE THE BALL: TO SOME DEGREE IT REALLY IS ALL IN YOUR HEAD

L et me just say here: You will only improve just so much with all the other steps I mention. You <u>must</u> address the mind directly! I can't stress this fact enough. You <u>must</u> improve the actual mechanisms within the mind that control how you feel. This is the final piece of the puzzle.

Back when my nerves were constantly shot, my psychiatrist suggested I try meditating as a form of relaxation. I was already aware of the possible benefits I could gain from meditating. Simply put, meditation is a powerful curative for just about anything that may ail you. The scientific community backs this fact. But I was too strung out to sit still for more than 10 seconds, let alone a half hour or more. However, I was interested that he would bring it up. He knew my meds were not working so he was willing to look into anything at all that might help me.

Almost a year passed before I came across the technique for meditating that I currently use. I discovered it unexpectedly. But the sales page caught my eye enough to want to know more. At this point in my bipolar experience I was becoming very desperate for any answers outside of the medical community. I was open to anything that might give me relief.

I was much better from having been on EMPowerPlus for some months, but I knew I was still missing an important piece to the puzzle. Purely intuition on my part, but I have learned to trust my gut in these matters. I also seem adept at finding answers to questions I wasn't even aware that I had.

DON'T FEEL LIKE PONDERING THE GREAT NOTHINGNESS? NO PROBLEM

D o yourself a big huge favor and head on over to **Centerpointe**. The founder **Bill Harris** developed a technical approach to meditation he calls **Holosync**. It addressed the issue of most people being unable to meditate for multiple reasons. It also addresses the time factor.

Achieving the life you want through meditation can take decades of many hours per day dedication. Bill's system boils it down to an hour a day across a handful of years. And the technology involved allows you to achieve an even deeper level of brain wave activity than is possible through traditional meditation. It just works better, faster. There literally are books written about Holosync so I will condense what I know down to the key points and what I personally have gained from using it.

First off and probably most important, if you have your headphones on, are sitting still with eyes closed, and are listening to the CDs—you are meditating and your life is improving. End of story. Anything you could possibly ask from here on out is secondary as far as results. If the sounds are going into your head, you are winning.

It does not matter if you can't hold still, if you fall asleep, if you can't stop thinking about anything and everything, if your leg itches and you scratch it, if you don't feel relaxed or think that anything is happening. None of that matters! *If you're listening, you're winning!* That is the key reason I bought my first set of CDs. You do not have to *feel* like you're meditating. That's not the point here. You're not after any sort of "experience" from the meditation sessions themselves, although some interesting things will probably take place. You are after the long-term good effects of listening to the CDs.

No need to worry about emptying your mind of all thoughts or the fact that nothing transcendental is taking place. None of that matters. What matters is what's changing in your mind. And it's not necessary to even judge how you think it's going for you. In fact, it's detrimental to do so. If you are faithfully listening every day or as close to every day as you can, your life is getting better. You'll be able to make better sense of it as you go. Don't even sweat it.

A LITTLE RELAXATION, A LITTLE REWIRING

A key part to this is your ability to stop fighting your situation in life. Your refusal to accept your lot in life is the key reason you feel so bad. This does NOT mean that you should cease trying to improve your life. It's more like being cool with the fact that you are right now doing all that you can to improve and you should take solace in that. Continue to try to fix the problems in your life but don't mentally stew in them. Stay positive.

I realize this is about a nigh impossible concept for most people to grasp. But Bill explains it exceedingly well in many ways after you have joined. And before you even commit, you can start reading helpful articles and blog posts explaining much of what Bill and Centerpointe help you with.

Just go to www.centerpointe.com and click on "ARTICLES" or "BLOG" and let the learning begin.

So what is it doing to your mind? Let's start with the mechanical. I found this part to be pretty trippy. Our brains work best if both halves are running at the same speed, vibrating at the same frequency. And the two halves need to be communicating to each other, sharing the load. But that is not how it is for most of us. Usually one side is dominating. It's taking care of most everything and it isn't talking to the other side. This causes us distress.

Holosync pumps two different frequencies into each ear. Imagine trying to follow two separate conversations from two different people talking into each ear at the same time. You can't follow both and completely understand what each is saying. Same with the Holosync frequencies. What happens is the mind takes the difference between the two frequencies and starts vibrating at the frequency that is the result. That in itself calms you down over time. The new frequency will match a target frequency equal to the level of brainwave activity found while meditating. That's a long way of saying, "You'll calm down."

The other thing taking place from this "forced confusion" is overload. You are sort of freaking out your brain. Throwing more at it than it can handle. But don't worry. It's not so much as to hurt you in any way. It's just enough that your brain is literally forced to rewire itself and form new neural pathways that will allow it to handle the stimulus of the CDs. Same thing as your body getting stronger from lifting weights. Over time you get stronger as the body adapts.

Well, over time your brain will grow new nerve cells and cause a new network of connections between all your neurons. This new network will be able to comfortably handle the stimulus of the CDs. They won't cause disruption any longer. In essence, your brain is stronger and more efficient.

What arises in your day-to-day life from this is a **higher threshold for dealing with stress.** You won't become upset as easily as before you started listening to the CDs. Your days will smooth out. You will have more patience with people who push your buttons. Your bad feelings and thoughts will start evaporating. I'm talking long term here but you may notice improvements happening right away. I did. Nothing stupendous. I just started feeling a little better in a general sense but it was a noticeable change to those close to me.

As you adapt and are able to handle what the CDs are causing in your mind, they become ineffective at causing further change. They are still relaxing you, but no new growth will occur. That's when you progress to the next lower set of frequencies. This is all planned out by Centerpointe. It will be made clear to you when you need to upgrade. And, you will NEVER be hit with the hard sell. That's not what they're about. Everything is handled at whatever pace is comfortable for you. Upgrade whenever you're able or whenever it feels right. Or don't upgrade at all. I don't suggest you not upgrading but as I said, you will get no grief from the support staff. Only help.

YOU NEED A NEW PLAN, MAN!

Now another interesting thing is happening right along with what I've told so far. This gets kind of deep so I'll just hit the highlights.

We all run our lives on a rule set we developed as children. This rule set does not account for much of how life is as an adult. But it's firmly in place and directing decisions we make all day long. To be blunt, it's screwing us up in many ways we're not even aware of. Holosync allows us to see the truth of how our thinking is harming us. It also gives us the ability to formulate a new set of rules that is better suited for here and now.

You slowly become able to see how you are probably shooting yourself in the foot throughout your day. You start developing a better method for making decisions. Because of that, your life gets better. You start getting more of what you want in your day. And you start choosing better things to want as well.

Your stress begins to be released. We all walk around with tension to some degree or another. And we all have pent up issues we may not even be aware of. These stresses can be stored anywhere in your body or mind. The technology causes this stuff to come out of you.

As you meditate you will probably be having a slew of thoughts. All kinds of thoughts. This is normal and good. These thoughts are one way your nervous system is doing a little house cleaning.

At any point in your day, including while you meditate, you might start feeling what would seem to be overly emotional. This is another way your system purges stress. It's called "upheaval." More house cleaning. But it passes. And when it does you feel better. Each time your body releases these stresses through upheaval, you are becoming closer to your ideal life.

You will be taught a new way to think. I don't mean in a doctrinal fashion. This is not a "my way is the right way" thing. It's more of an efficiency upgrade kind of thing. Whatever you focus on you will draw into your life. Good or bad. It's called "The Law of Attraction." Your powerful subconscious mind is always at work trying to bring to you what you ask of it, so to speak. You have to learn to be careful with what you are asking of it.

If you consistently maintain positive thoughts, you will probably have a happier life than most. But just like a powerful computer, it only knows what data you are typing into it. It is not aware of your feelings about the data or what you really meant when you input that data. It only knows the data.

If you constantly think about what you do NOT want, your subconscious can't tell the difference. It will work just as hard to bring that negative into your life. It only knows that that is what you are thinking about. It doesn't discriminate between negative and positive. Therefore, you *must* change the way you think.

If you wish your life was better or there is something you'd like to achieve but haven't, it can be directly tied to the way you think. You need a new way.

PRINT 'EM OUT AND STACK 'EM NEAR THE BOWL

As I pointed out earlier, on the Centerpointe website you will find the helpful articles and blog posts. If you don't want to read them off your screen, then just print them out to read offline in a way that is more comfortable. I know when I was bipolar, the act of screen reading would sometimes enrage me. No idea why. Just did. I've since learned that others feel this way too, sometimes.

Bill Harris is a trip to listen to and read. He's just a guy who figured something out that works. He did it to save his own self years ago. He too was leading a less than stellar existence and he'll be the first to tell you that. He was almost forty before he figured out how to fix his life.

He isn't presenting any new ideas as far as meditation and life improvement go. He just figured out an easier way for all of us to attain the results these areas cover. But he writes and speaks in a way that I think you will enjoy. He's funny and very intelligent. He talks straight.

He goes to massive lengths to help you understand how you can feel better and have the life you dream about. If you're way down in the hole and just want to feel better, then go to Centerpointe. They have a help desk staffed with great folks who will take all the time you need to start learning how they can help you feel better. The help desk is a free service.

I cannot stress enough how important finding Centerpointe has been for me. Truehope got me on stable ground. They are number one on my list but Centerpointe is definitely the very next step you should take to feel better. I look at Truehope as the rescue raft that pulled me from the ocean of hopelessness just before I sank. Centerpointe is the shoreline of the country I have spent my life trying to reach.

I could spend months talking about Centerpointe alone and never cover everything they address. The mind is a weighty subject. Bill has an incredible amount of material to share and everyone needs to hear all of it, bipolar or not. Spirituality plays a big part in his company but he does not endorse any one belief system. There is nothing on his site that could possibly offend anyone in this area.

You must address the way you think. This is covered extensively in the newsletters and the support letters you will regularly receive when you begin the process. You must address the way you speak to yourself inside. You must develop the ability to objectively (free from emotion) witness your life and actions, which will enable you to improve your decision-making process for the better. These are all integral parts to why you have bipolar disorder. It's why you are where you are in your life. Really, it's why any of us are who we are.

Well, I wasn't too happy with whom I was and I accepted that if I wanted a better life then I had to develop a new way of thinking. The life I had was one derived from every decision I'd ever made prior to becoming better. That process never changes, but now I work hard to think like a person does who has the kind of life I want. That just makes sense to me. Wish I'd've figured it out a couple of decades sooner. But I guess we figure things out when the time is right and that's that with that.

HORROR NOVEL WRITERS SLEEP LIKE BABIES

Another daily task that has brought me relief is to keep a journal. I write down anything and everything in that bad boy. I have a few different reasons why I do this and they don't all pertain to feeling better. But that was the reason I first had in mind when I picked up my shiny new notebook at Office Depot. I had to get it out.

I started writing my thoughts while going through my second divorce. Matter of fact that was pretty much the only thing I ever wrote about for months. It seemed to occupy much of my mental faculties at the time. Much. But it helped.

It's not good to keep all your crap inside. I logged in a bunch of entries dealing with my state of mind. It helped me to make sense of my thoughts too. Something special happens when you write. Your mind gets engaged in helping itself as your eyes watch the words spill out onto the paper. It becomes therapy.

You need to SEE what your mind is chewing on. The more you write as days go by, the better you feel. Not right away by any stretch, but you start to get a good feel about what you spend all your energy on. What you're focusing on. This then helps you to decide if you should, in fact, keep focusing on these things or consider some better topics. Your thoughts will organize.

As the months went by I began to write of things other than my divorce. Just a little here and there about my fight with the bipolar, how my physical health was, my new goals, hikes I took in the mountains, movies I enjoyed— whatever. But I got it all out. Interestingly, this was something else my psychiatrist agreed was a good thing to do.

I laughingly told him how I meant it to be a way to put down my thoughts and decide on what to do with my life, but in reality it was turning into my "Divorce Logbook" as I called it. That's all I seemed to write about. He said it didn't matter. The whole idea of the journal was nothing but beneficial. Told me to write whatever I wanted, that it would make me feel better. He was right.

Now I do write about my various goals. I also write down what I am grateful for every day. I learned that this is something successful people do but that everyone should do it regardless as it enables you to appreciate life more. You take nothing for granted. Some days I only have one or two items to list. Other days I write pages.

So write! It's simply one more inexpensive but highly valuable tool you can use to make yourself well. Nobody's grading you and you never have to share it with anyone, ever. Write one sentence, write a novel. If you're happy, write about it. If you are feeling hateful or want to destroy something, write about it. It doesn't matter what you write. But do it and see where it takes you. You might be surprised.

GET YOUR ASS IN GEAR!

Exercise. Gotta do it. Remember how I noticed I felt better if I kept moving when a panic attack struck? I believe that is a potent indication of how much good exercise can help. Really. You should be exercising anyway, even if you're not bipolar. Your body is designed to move. It functions better when it is in motion.

Too much sitting around or lying in bed causes your system to become sluggish. Nutrients, oxygen, and water don't get delivered properly to the cells. Waste products and toxins build up inside of you and don't get shuttled out fast enough, if at all, before they do harm to you.

There is a compounding effect. As your body becomes inefficient your mind follows suit. And for this crowd, that is a disaster. I'll repeat it: You MUST take care of your body if you want any hope of fixing your mind. You must!

I know from personal experience that it is tough to exercise when you are depressed. It can be seemingly impossible to go to a gym and face the public while simultaneously not looking your best. Ultimately, getting into the gym would be best. Realistically, that can be a humungous step many of us don't want to face. So take your time. No need to be gym bound before it's feasible.

Start walking around town first. Go for hikes in the outdoors if it's available. Begin with pushups, crunches, and leg raises in the home (no situps—murderous on the back in the long run). Start jogging or speed walking. Ride a bike. Go swimming if the season's right.

I also am aware that this is a difficult task for anybody to undertake but again—for us it is mandatory. The deck is stacked against us. You should feel even more compelled than the sane folks to want to improve your physical health. You don't have to pursue bodybuilding if you don't want to. That's a whole other commitment level in itself. But the basics should be looked into.

Join a gym, regardless. There are fewer gym rats and more average citizenry in there these days anyhow. Unless you live near a hardcore gym. But you'd know right away if you just walked into the wrong doorway for your current fitness needs. They smell blood. And fear. Like the gym I wrote about earlier. So look for a fitness center type of place.

Don't feel self-conscious. The big guys do not care what you look like. Even in a fitness center they are too busy getting huge to even notice you. It's a whole other level of focus and concentration, believe me.

Bodybuilding or not, the exercises are all the same. Just the end goals are different. Find out how to do them properly if you are new. If you lift wrong you can cripple yourself or at the very least develop some nagging issues in your joints and spine. Avoid that.

Talk to the gym owner. Any owner worth his salt is going to want to know what you need and want from his facility. Then he's going to point you in the right direction. That's just good business. He'll tell you.

If you're able, hire a trainer. Once you have the basics down pat you can train yourself from there. You only need a trainer to get you going or if you decide you want to excel, then you may need him/her again to advance a level. But for general good health, just get the basics and repeat them over time. As long as you are working your body, it will be happy.

I've already told you the best supplements to have on hand for your mind and they apply to repairing the exercising body as well. The only others to add would be maybe creatine (which is totally safe by the way, should you have heard different) for muscle growth/strength, and glucosamine sulfate to assist joint health. Not a fix but an assist.

A beautiful resource to study that is operated by a man with impeccable credentials and honesty is Body Building Revealed. It can be found at this link:

http://www.musclebuildingnutrition.com/cgi/at.cgi?a=436438

You will save thousands by not getting ripped off by the supplement companies! This site shows how and it applies to all levels of fitness.

LEMME 'SPLAIN A FEW THINGS

Exercise will help you allay your symptoms. You may remember how I learned that lactic acid from hard exercise causes symptoms to appear for some of us. It did so strongly in me. But now I have the added benefit of what I have learned since. I can now train hard with no resulting symptoms. If you are doing everything else I wrote about prior to beginning your training, you won't even experience what I did. Back then I didn't have all the good things I learned about to provide the foundation I needed so that the lactic acid couldn't harm me. Now I do and I train hard and I am okay.

There is one possible exception you may face. May. It's been found that in some individuals, the psychotropic medication can still be present in minute amounts within your body. It seems to like to attach to protein more so than fat, although it can be in fat too. The residue will store in your muscles and oddly enough, your lungs. There's a speculative reason why but this is just a "so you know" kind of deal.

Intense exercise can cause these toxic residuals to release back into your bloodstream, effectively overmedicating you. Instantly. There is documented proof of this on Truehope's website. They recommend that should such a thing occur, you quickly consume either hydrolized whey protein or BCAAs (branched chain amino acids). Either of these nutrients will attach to the residue and form a particle too large to pass through the blood/brain barrier. Your body will then eliminate the particles. This is rare I believe, but possible.

So go into your training very easy and in a controlled fashion. See what's what. Dip your toe in the water first. Build up intensity slowly over a couple of months and just see how you feel. You would do that anyway just to train correctly. If you're OK, well then, you're OK! If you feel odd, immediately stop and judge what you think may be causing it. If your mind/body is telling you it's meds, then slam some whey or BCAA's immediately.

Assuming all is well, stay active. Exercise also produces the happy hormones in your head. They are a stress response to help you survive. As you push yourself physically, your body produces these brain chemicals to relieve some of the pain so that you can continue. It's just a machine trained for survival. It doesn't know that you're simply exercising to feel better. It only knows how to survive. So you win by experiencing the pleasant side effect of mood-lifting hormones entering your bloodstream. <u>You will feel better</u>. <u>You will feel better</u>. <u>You will feel better</u>.

As your training stretches on, you will begin to physically look better as well. That then makes you feel even better yet! It's a big part of why everybody trains. For those of us here, it can be a minor lifesaver in itself. Anything you do to improve your life will improve your mental state. As you feel better you will also be strikingly aware that you made it happen. You are in control! This will do wonders for your whole outlook. Trust me on this.

If you have any physical handicaps—old injuries, bad back, high blood pressure, trick knee—you will have to develop an appropriate training regime. Stay within your limits. You don't need an extra problem on top of the nice stack you may already have. Start out slow and easy. If you've been sedentary for any length of time, the machine will protest. Go easy for the first few weeks and let the body adapt to the new stimulus. And it will adapt.

If you do decide to lift weights, you will be very sore. On the sore days either rest or do aerobics. Any kind. Stationary bike, treadmill, walking, you get the picture. Your goals will determine how much, what type, and how intensely to do it. Walking doesn't do much of anything for fat burning or cardiovascular health. But it does do a little bit. The best thing about it or any other low-level aerobics exercise is that it will help to keep you limber on the non-lifting days.

Toxins that build up due to the inflammation caused by weightlifting can collect in the body. Some light aerobics will get the juices flowing, literally, and help your body heal faster. As your muscle fibers heal their minute tears from lifting, you can become a little stiff. Besides stretching, low-level aerobics will help keep you loose. Keeping your blood flowing isn't just about toxin removal either. Fresh blood will keep your healing muscles covered in a soup of nutrients and oxygen. You'll heal faster.

There is so much I could say about training and the different types for different goals. Start with what I've just shared if you are brand new. I'll have more to share in future books. If you used to lift and got side lined as I did, don't eat your ass up about being away from the iron pile. Shit happens. Just get back in there. You will find as I did that muscle memory is an incredible thing!

JUST GIVE IT TO ME STRAIGHT!

A nd now for the clarification round! The next chapter shows my system laid out in the order I used to get better that was most comfortable for me. <u>I am not sharing theory. I have lived or still live these steps to get and stay well</u>. Except for the first three, you may mix up the steps in whatever order works best for you. Many factors affect what is or isn't convenient for all of us as we proceed through this list. Consider all steps, do the first three in order, then go with your gut on the rest. But don't leave any out.

KEN JENSEN

YOU'VE PAID THE TOLL AND NOW CAN ENTER NORMAL CITY!

IT'S TIME WE APPLIED A GOOD BEATING TO THIS DEMON

I call my system "TORQUE² BACK." It's an easy to remember acronym for the eleven steps of my system. But it's befitting of what's going to take place for you and your life. Up until this point in time, you have been dragged to ever-lower levels of existence. You have seen less and less light and more and more dark.

Now you will begin to pull your mind back from the edge of the abyss. You're going to apply pressure to the disease. You're going to lock on to your mind with the torque wrench I have provided and start heaving it in the proper direction. Your bipolar is going to lose its grip. It's going to buckle under the force of your burgeoning good health.

You are going to learn how to use my tools like a professional mechanic.

You are going to learn how to fight like a Marine.

You are going to take charge of your life and become the person you were meant to be.

You will do all of these things just as I did and you will find the same joy and peace as I have found.

While an acronym makes it easier to remember the actual steps, it doesn't exactly lay them out in the order you need to follow. Not the first three, anyhow. So pay attention: The first three steps are absolutely critical and must be followed in the order in which I present them. But here's a little bonus for you: Doing step one and two, which entails all of swallowing some capsules, will make it much easier to do step three.

Simply <u>beginning</u> step three will make all the rest of the steps doable in time, if they seem too hard. None of this needs to be a struggle and if you follow my system, it will come to life on its own. You will not have to manifest some Conan-like fortitude. It will gradually appear if you stay consistent. Trust me and relax. Please.

(T)ruehope

Go to <u>www.truehope.com</u> **first.**

To get signed up as a participant you'll need to call the help desk:

1-888-878-3467. Tell them that Ken Jensen sent you and ask them how you should proceed. Everyone is different and you <u>have to</u> speak with a counselor to make sure the best program is designed for your specific needs. It is <u>critical</u> that you speak with their counselors. Don't worry. They are very, very friendly people!

(O)megabrite
Go to <u>www.omegabrite.com</u> **second.**

They have a very simple order form but you can phone them at:
1-800-383-2030
I use 6 gels per day so a box lasts me ten days. So I order three boxes each month. You can use more or less. The omegas are the second most crucial nutrient beyond everything you should be taking via Truehope.

(R)elax with Centerpointe
Go to http://www.centerpointe.com **third.**

They have an extremely helpful customer service department:
1-800-945-2741 for U.S residents and
1-503-673-7117 for folks outside of the U.S.
They can be reached 24/7. The online order form is easy to use too.

(Q)uit addictions

(U)nacceptable stressors must be removed
Make the tough calls and change what must be
changed in your world for you to be sane.

(E²) Eat right and Exercise

(B)e OK with the fact that you are right where you're meant to be for now, which is on the path to better health!

(A)ddress physical ailments

(C)hat which is to say **TALK** to someone about what's on your mind

(K)eep a journal

And there you have it. I tried to stick to the most relevant topics and experiences from my life that pertained to my bipolar disorder. Unlike Hunter S. Thompson, drugs did not always work for me. (Hunter is one of my favorite anti-heroes. Google him if he's new to you. Enjoy the ride.)

But I believe that much of my partying was directly connected to my illness. Chemicals were the relief from, then the cause of my problems. That is true for everyone who imbibes but I doubt many of them are left with bipolar disorder in the end. I know I was experiencing symptoms long before I was ever diagnosed. I was just too numb to realize it or whenever I did feel weird I mislabeled the cause.

I self-medicated like a son of a gun! I can remember times when I felt "too good." How can you feel too good? Now I realize I was becoming manic. This was years before the major fun began. I'd say two thirds of my life was not handled properly. I hurt myself and many close to me frequently over the years. Now I can see why that may have been.

I used to be buried in guilt and shame from some of the things I've done. At times I thought those two emotions alone would destroy me. I did many things that I will take to the grave. No one who knows me knows everything. I often could not fathom bearing the loads I did for much longer. Somehow I was able.

I used to have some mighty huge regrets. Some I carried for decades. But I changed all that. I can't take back what I did and I did some incredibly bad things here and there. But I've punished myself more than enough. Dwelling on any of it fixes nothing. Whatever price I feel I may have owed to the Universe has been paid in full. Now I look at all of it as a learning experience. "Let's make sure we don't go down THAT road again".

I have shown you the exact steps I took to get my life back and more. My life has never been this good. Never. I have a sense of wellness I have never had before. As of this writing, I still get a little taste of the darkness once in awhile; a moment of impending panic, an odd sensation sprinting across the mental front lawn. But it is very minimal and very sporadic. It is almost nonexistent. I will never say that I am cured but I am off all medication. That is why I say I beat it.

Maybe I can't win the war but I'm winning the battles on a consistent basis. I am completely against the use of medication as a long-term option to treating bipolar disorder. Our country uses the most amounts of meds and yet we are among the sickest people of the world. Do the math. My life and that of others like me has amply proven to me that meds are not the way to go. I believe this applies to much more than just bipolar disorder but I have to specifically stick with the area in which I have direct experience. That is only fair. I offer no medical advice. But my psychiatrist agrees wholeheartedly with me. He thinks if there is a way I can feel better that involves no medication, then that is the best way to go.

I mentioned earlier that you should not just lie back with your diagnosis as a bipolar individual and accept that as the way it will be. That is the **victim** mentality and it leads to ultimate ruin. It may be necessary to acknowledge your diagnosis and make sure those closest to you understand that you have a huge fight on your hands in a day to day fashion that most never experience. These people need to know that you will need some room to operate. From there **you must take responsibility for your life.**

I offer much here to help you and it all works but it is going to require a fighting spirit on your end. Don't view yourself as a helpless victim. You're up against the wall right now but you CAN break free. You just have to want it bad enough and have a good plan in place to launch your campaign. Ultimately only YOU can help yourself. I'm just providing the proper tools and proof based on my hairy life that it can be done.

I wholeheartedly believe that you need a good foundation to begin your healing. That foundation is proper nutrition, in particular **Truehope**. Nothing else will help you until you address this main issue. You can then proceed from there in addressing all other tangible factors you can control. As good as all the other info is that I've shared with you regarding health and nutrition, you MUST address the actual functioning of your mind. The physical aspects of brain function must be made as efficient as possible. Your brain must be treated like a high-end sports car. Ultimately you want it to function at that level.

Secondly, you must address the way you direct your thoughts. My Grandpa used to say, "Wherever you go, there you are." He was right. You have thought your way into whatever stage of life you currently experience. If you're not happy with that experience then it is up to you to do something about it. That's where **Holosync** and **Bill Harris'** teachings come into play. In its simplest form the brain is just one more machine. Optimize its performance and a great life is the reward.

I know that I will have to remain vigilant in my monitoring of my health. I have accepted that I will have to always take extra steps that "normal" people don't have to worry about in order to have a healthy and happy life. But you know what? There is an unforeseen **benefit** to all of this. My life has become better in ways that extend way beyond just relieving my symptoms. I have a sense of hope and a purpose in life that I have been searching for, for decades. It feels fantastic! As you use the steps I've outlined I believe the same will happen for you.

Your immediate goal of just feeling better, obtaining some relief, will in fact, take place. But as you continue your self-treatment your eyes will see things you've been overlooking. Your life will become more enriched. People will like being around you more. You will cross paths with others who can help you or simply make life more fun and interesting for having met each other. You will think your way into a bigger and better life. What I'm trying to say here is that you're just gonna have to come to terms with the fact that life is way better than you ever imagined and that you will experience this upgraded lifestyle by default.

Maybe you recognize something about yourself or someone you know, in me. I meet people almost every day who know someone who is bipolar and then tell me the related horror story. I recognize my old self as they speak and I hurt for the afflicted person. I also understand the position it puts family and friends in. It's very hard on them as well. That is an understatement.

This is a hard illness to get the healthy to comprehend. It's frustrating to both sides. Unfortunately, this disease is becoming prevalent enough that more and more people are becoming familiar with it. Maybe that's a good thing. As more people are forced to deal with it, better treatments will arise and systems like mine will become better known and accepted. I think many of us can see that the established methods are not working. It's time you take a new perspective on your treatment. Time to send in the Marines!

KEN JENSEN

SO THEN WHAT HAPPENED?

SIT WHILST I WAX ELOQUENT

I decided to add this extra summation almost two years after this project began for me. Folks wanted to know more about how life's been treating me as I continue to follow the steps in my own system. So, the following batch of facts is presented in no specific order, but will give you a clear picture on how better and sweeter life has become for both me, and anyone who regularly interacts with me.

Nicotine is out. As of this writing, it's been one year since I stopped chewing tobacco and about three since I quit smoking. It was hard to do, at first, but the reward of feeling as good as I do now, has been well worth it.

No urges to get high, drunk, or self-medicate. Another Godsend. I've been plagued most of my life with a need to have at least *something* in me at all times; something to take off the edge of life. The older I got, the more I hated this aspect of my personality. I felt weak and controlled. No more. I still can't linger in front of a beer display as it would look too beautiful and refreshing but it's a weak sensation and it evaporates in seconds.

I fear getting high, drunk, or self-medicating. My body and mind both, have made it painfully clear to me that to throw anything down the hatch that doesn't belong, will result in swift and brutal punishment in the form of devastating panic and feelings of sickness. I behave because the outcome of not doing so couldn't possibly be less worth it.

I am never bored! A huge part of all my imbibing and dysfunction was from being bored. I had to fill the time or forget that it was passing. I wasted so many years just getting ripped while accomplishing nothing else, whatsoever. Today, I am so busy with all that I do, I never get bored. This is a state of existence I have hoped and prayed for as far back as I can remember. Boredom is pointless and to me, painful.

I have a purpose. The aforementioned boredom came from two things; being forced (as I saw it) to lead a life I didn't want, which encompassed my entire life, and simply not knowing what the hell I was actually supposed to be doing with my time to avoid it. It has taken me just shy of forty years to figure out what I want to be when I grow up, but I am now doing it. This is satisfying beyond words.

I manage my time better. Time management is only a problem when you have too much to do. I never had too much to do until this project kicked off. I have worked many hours at jobs in the past but not much else was happening at home to make time management a problem. I have learned to make lists, prioritize tasks, and set goals: immediate, mid range, and long term. This is a success secret I took from Arnold Schwarzenegger. I couldn't be more serious. You can't map out your route if you don't even know where you're going. And to know where you're going, you need a route. I've learned to utilize both and my life got better for it.

I still take meds for physical health. I am against all meds for treating bipolar and depression but physical health is different. Some issues must be addressed with meds. But even then, a doctor has to present a pretty compelling reason why I should take what they recommend and you can bet your paycheck I will be researching healthier ways around it. But until I find that way, I take the meds I must. I have high blood pressure issues in my family and high cholesterol issues too. I also have an underactive thyroid that keeps me from maintaining my girlish figure so I have no choice but to address that medicinally. For now. Ha-ha! Ever the bull-headed one am I.

My overall aim in life; what I'm building. This book is but one part of a much larger goal. I have a drive to succeed that is ferocious. Always has been but it took me this long to learn how to pull it off. In the past, I only wanted to make a pile of cash and enjoy life. That hasn't changed but something's been added.

I learned the hard way, that it is impossible for me to get what I want in life if I don't help someone else get what they need in life. It has also been important to realize that I have to want to help people. You can help people and not really care. You can do a lot of good but not really care. To get what I want out of this life, I have to do good **and** I have to care. The caring part is what amplifies the sweetness of the whole deal; makes it more fun, more satisfying, and ensures it will actually happen. I had to learn what I really cared about. Right now, that's you reading this book. I want you to have what I have!

My work day. Every morning I sit down with my coffee and go through everything that may have changed or needs responding to since yesterday. Then I whip up a huge fitness shake; fruit, OJ, milk, whey protein, glutamine, creatine, and glucosamine sulfate, and start working through that as I answer questions from all who wrote me.

I'll then head to the gym for a vicious workout or run errands, or I'll begin writing and addressing technical issues for my business. Except for eating and cooking, that is my whole day from there on out. I sometimes take hikes in the woods but I don't socialize, as yet.

Every other weekend, I get my son and I do my best to give him a nice weekend with his Dad.

At the end of the day, I decompress with a DVD, as I don't watch much TV at all.

So most of my day, every day, is spent on my computer. For now. I am a big believer in outsourcing and look forward to the day when all I do is write and speak with people. For now, I do it all.

People who knew the "old me" can see the change for the better in the "new me." For one, I've dropped about 75 pounds of fat and added about ten pounds of muscle. I went from blob to athletic. It's a big change. But the wildest thing is my eyes and facial expressions. I was told I either looked "drugged" or "sinister" most days. Either way, no one really wanted to approach me.

The other thing was people used to see a crazy energy in my eyes. It portended danger. I looked like something bad about to happen. It was different from my "sinister" look. It was more of a "madman" affair. Like I was getting excited about something that most wouldn't. A bad something. That's all gone.

People approach me and talk to me, freely. I was isolated from the world for years even when surrounded by people. It is a loneliness that can kill you. It has a crushing presence. People wanted nothing to do with me. When I talked to them, they did all they could to end the meeting fast. My jokes fell flat. My sense of humor was often improper. Or sometimes I'd just start sharing violent stories from my past or how I'd handle something with violence right now, just in idle conversation. I was in some dark, scary reality that I could not always keep to myself and even if I did, people could pick up on it and wanted nothing to do with me.

Now, people smile when I enter a room. People don't get that "deer in the headlights look" when I walk past them and say hi. They respond in a normal fashion. Sometimes, if I'm tired or ticked off, I can still cause people to veer away as they see me coming. But that's only when I choose to subtlely advertise that I want to be left alone. I can launch the "look" at pushy salespeople with great effectiveness in stores. But it's a choice now, not an involuntary fact.

I am making new friends by the truckload! Based on what I just shared above, you can see how lonely life got for me. I missed people! I missed people caring about me even if just out of politeness. I hated being ignored. I hated that people never knew how to respond to seemingly any damn thing I had to say. I got better, and people like me now. It's been a few years and it hasn't got old yet!

I freely meet new people and say hello, go out of my way to introduce myself, put them at ease if they can't seem to find the social opening to do so themselves. It feels awesome to be liked again! I work very, very hard on gauging my actions when I deal with people and do my best to change where I must or when to not say something I'd normally say, just so people feel comfortable when meeting me. It's not "kissing up" or manipulation. It's the fact that I can come on too strong in a number of ways and I learned I very easily freak people out without trying. I'm too intense many times. I still am but I learned tact and I learned how to just do the social dance a lot better. It makes my day and theirs, far more pleasant for having met me. I do this in written communications too. Cripes, I try anyway.

I found the root of everything that is "me." In my search for constant improvement, I discovered Garrett Loporto's "The Da Vinci Method." I discovered the real me in its entirety. It explained why "normal," "average," and "regular" life sucks the soul right out of me and why I have been and still am, hard pressed to fight against that way of thinking and living. It explained the biggest root cause for why I've ever done anything like I have and why it led to my becoming bipolar. It was a relief to read his words. I need more out of this life than what most are willing to settle for and it turns out, that's a good thing and it is my "normal."

Truehope got even better! What I'm about to share did not exist when I first began working with Truehope. The website changed drastically and for the better. The homepage offers far more than it used to. And now they have a portfolio of brochures, very professional in appearance, designed to appeal to all the people in your world as you fight bipolar.

There's one specifically to give to your doctor, explaining the whats and whys of Truehope; one for any to read explaining the same; a support person's guide to help them help a sick person; and a participant guide to help you understand how you can help yourself. I was ecstatic when I got my first set of these. What a great help for everyone involved!

Physique and physical health are in stellar form. I had severe back pain for a few years. It was from a number of issues. I have much damage in my spine but I found that as I fixed my bipolar problems, I was once again able to train hard in the gym. I'm 40 right now, so I have limits I've never had, but I can train around them easily and I'm no longer driven by my ego as I was when I was younger. I protect myself from injury like never before. And the reward has been a physique of the kind I've always dreamed. Not perfect, not magazine material, but massively satisfying for my needs.

Somehow, I have suffered no permanent damage from all the years of drugs, drinking, smoking, and bad eating. My heart has been tested and my blood is routinely checked. I have high blood pressure and high cholesterol, both of which stay normal as I take my meds for them. But that stuff runs in my family and with all I've been through, I am truly amazed that that is all I have wrong with me!

My sleep leveled out. The more time passes by and the more fulfilling my life becomes, the less sleep I seem to need. Waking up is still a painful experience both physically and mentally. I don't enjoy it but I am able to do it. For years, I loathed alarm clocks. I had an intense hatred for them. But now that my life has purpose and responsibilities again, I am able to get up when I need to. That has been a major victory for me.

Air Hunger. The one thorn left in my side. I had a recurrence of waking up unable to swallow, and feeling as if I hadn't been breathing. I would wake up with my heart hammering hard in my chest, I mean brutally hard, and feeling very scared, disoriented, and thinking I couldn't breathe or that my heart was going to stop. This used to happen to me regularly when my symptoms first appeared but then went away for years. It's since returned.

Here's what happened: I asked my medical doctor, my psychiatrist, Centerpointe, and Truehope. They had no answers, nor any similar stories from others. I had a meeting with a sleep study doctor and we agreed that this is not Sleep Apnea. But even then, <u>he</u> didn't even know what it was! I finally asked my chiropractor what he thought this might be. He was the only one who felt sure enough to offer an opinion.

It's unhashed, unresolved stresses still lingering in my mind and body. He told me that as I continue on the path I've taken, I will learn to resolve this. And it's looking like he was right. I still have this problem but it has been steadily getting weaker and appearing less.

It affects me when I'm awake, too. I feel like not enough air is getting into my lungs and it causes me to yawn and inhale as deep as possible. This is sporadic and seems to be directly connected to what's going on in my day. However, the awake version weakens and is sporadic, as well.

I have also learned how to control it better. I realized through experience, that nothing's really wrong. It's a form of panic, I feel. So I can calm myself and force it to eventually disperse. I know that as I continue to meditate with Centerpointe, this too shall pass. Google the term "air hunger" and see what you find. Lots of talk but no explanation. Well, I just explained it to you. (I think.)

I am great friends with my former alcohol and drug counselors. Not too long ago, I gave a talk at the very group I used to mandatorily attend after my last DWI. My counselor was still there and very happy to see the improvement. I was a hit at the talk. The group of all guys was very pissed off, just like I was when I was a member. But I left them laughing and gave them some insight from a "street level" perspective. I didn't talk to them like a regular counselor. I talked to them as an equal, although I am no longer actively hooked on anything. My counselors said I am nothing like when they first met me and were pleased with the talk I gave.

I am even better friends with my Probation Officer. This fact actually cracks me up. I had one P.O. who later admitted to me that she thought at any moment, I was going to come across the desk and rip her throat out. Her words.

I got switched to a P.O. going for her Master's degree in social services specializing in mental illness. This woman was too damn chipper for her own good and constantly irritated me in the beginning of our relationship. She really pissed me off by always ending our meetings with the question, "Any police activity? Any drug use or alcohol use?" This is her job but I felt I'd made it abundantly clear that I knew my deal and that I no longer would do those things. It was insulting to my intelligence and esteem that she'd keep asking.

I set her on a new path one day by telling her, "X, if I ever were to drink again, you'd already have been notified by the police who jailed me. It is impossible for me to drink and not go full-on psychotic and raging. If I drink, half the county's emergency services will alert you to it. You won't need to ask me. And we'd be having this conversation through bars."

She accepted that and stopped asking me. I then got her involved with my book and website and due to her schooling, I have very in-depth, mutually beneficial discussions on all issues pertaining to people like me and what I'm doing business-wise.

She showed me an email she sent out to her superiors stating that, from talking to me, she has entirely changed how she treats others like me, for the better. She routinely sends people to my website, whom she thinks would benefit from my knowledge, both clients and other professionals like her. How's that for The Good Housekeeping Seal of Approval? And by the time you've read this, I will probably have been a free man again for quite some time.

What my psychiatrist told me last. This was one of the sweetest moments of my life. My doc went way out of his way to help me get on disability. Long after I'd stopped all meds, I still visited him, every few months, just to update him and because I thought I was supposed to for disability.

Turns out, I didn't have to. I asked and he said, "Don't worry, I'll cover whatever requirements the state has in confirming your need to stay on the books until you no longer need to." He knows I cannot go back to work. More on that in a moment.

During my last visit, he took off his glasses, looked at me, and said, "I don't know why you keep coming to see me. You don't need to. **Whatever you're doing is clearly working great.** Do you feel you even *need* to talk to me further? Because I am **no longer** concerned about you. I **don't worry** about you anymore. You're **fine** and you're going to **stay** that way. It's up to you if you still want to do checkups but I don't see the point.

How happy did that little exchange make Kenny?

Because of the position he's in professionally, he can't publicly vouch for my system, but he told me emphatically that he is very happy for me. He told me I was some kind of f***** up individual in the past and between the violence I exhibited and worshipped, and the behavior, he feared I'd be dead soon. He is amazed and happy for my turnaround but can't vouch for it. But I respect him still, I always enjoyed talking with him and he was a huge help, regardless.

Disability and my returning to work. The government saved my bacon. Disability was a draining and stressful fight to win but I needed it. I'm still on it now, as I build all that I am. Although my symptoms are gone, I cannot hold a job. Jobs were part of the fuel for the illness.

I used to get frustrated as I constructed my dream and I thought about finding a job in an attempt to out earn disability and speed up my business growth. I shared this with my younger brother one day.

"I keep thinking about getting a job and speeding up this whole thing." He said, "Yeah, you could do that. But what are you gonna do after *that* 47 minutes is up?" And then we laughed.

He's right. I can't do it. I can't. I can work intensely on what's mine but I can't ever be an employee again. I have had the same exact discussion with my folks. Kind of searching for the "adults" take on this, if you will, from the people who know me best. Dad, a man of few words, just shook his head, "Nope. You're all done with that. You're all done. Besides, you're doing what you do and you're meant for it. You'll be fine but you ain't ever going back to work. Just not your thing." Ma says about the same thing.

My first ex, who still advises me whether I want to hear it or not, puts it a little more bluntly, "What're you, nuts? I mean more nuts than you already are?

Bwaaa! You can't go back to work. You'll melt down or kill somebody. Don't be so stupid! Build your business." You have to know her like I do to understand why I appreciate that. And she's right. She usually is. Dammit.

But I'll tell you this—I want off disability. It saved me, big time, but it's not where I want to be. Just getting the check each month is demoralizing, symbolically. It's not that disability is bad; it's that I should and could be doing better. And I hate being dependent on an institution like this. It's no better than having an employer; too inflexible, with no possibility for growth.

I'm becoming a great dad. Once my son arrived, I constantly feared not doing right by him. I couldn't handle the responsibility, but I wanted so badly for him to be all right and not be somehow screwed up through my doings. Well, he's six right now and we are tight. He loves me and I love him. I don't get to see him much but he is constantly in the back of my mind. I teach him a lot about the outdoors and I'm very patient and creative when I'm explaining something to him.

I don't really care what he wants to do with his life either, as long as it's healthy and good. I'd be right out of my mind with pride (in a good way) if he were to become a Marine, like his dad, but if not, that's cool, too.

I just want him to be healthy and happy, like any good father, but when I was sick, I couldn't even muster up those feelings. I am glad I have them, and him, now.

I am doing what I do for me, first and foremost, because that's the only way it'll work, but once I have built up my dream, I want to use it to further his dreams and one day leave it all to him as my legacy.

Relationships. My two marriages taught me a ton about women and even more about myself. I am much clearer on what I want in a mate and I am much clearer in how wrong I've been as a husband. I am talking beyond the obvious mismatch both marriages were. There were still many things I could've handled better. Even aside from the illness, which made me pure evil to both women more than once, I just could've been a better person. I stay alone now, as I build my dream, as it's easier and kinder to both me and the future other half of "us" but I think hard on what the next girl will be like and how I'm gonna act.

I know everything can't be perfect and not all the marital discord was my fault, but I know I can do better in the future. I just can. Both my wives taught me that much. And I believe both of them were perfect for me for where and who I was at those times.

The Internet is a battleground and your cash is the prize. I have come to despise the words/phrases/tactics: guru, Internet Marketing, MLM,

Network Marketing, take away tactics in emails or sales pages, massive bonuses for signing up or buying, anything that purports to be easy or "we'll do the work for you," anything mentioning a "downline," the phrase "we'll put people under you," the word "automatic" used in any sense, investment opps, HYIPs, affiliates, looking for agents, in just (insert brief time frame) you can…yada, yada, yada, offers for softwares that I simply MUST have to be efficient/profitable, enlightening/self-help books consisting of generalities and fluff, the barrage of cross promotion between marketers as they all promote the newest "launch," etc., etc., etc.

This is but a small sampling of all I've fallen for or pursued, usually while manic AND depressed about my lack of cash, and have since learned to filter from my life.

What kills me is I have to use some variance of a few of these to get my message to people, too. I just can't stand being lumped in with the rest.

But if you're still sick and pondering how to get ahead in this life, then look carefully at the above list and wean yourself from this useless and potentially dangerous clutter.

I've learned, after spending around $50,000 of cash I never really had, that you have to build something that's yours and do so with sensible help from professionals. Much of this will still be trial and error. Go easy. Be careful, as I do now.

My thinking has changed. I see things globally now. I don't mean just with other nations. I see other people's points of view. I realize more than ever before, life is not black and white. It's shades of grey.

I am able to make friends with people who would not be friends with each other if all three of us were together. I always was good at that, lost it while bipolar, and got it back. But it came back bigger.

My own decision-making processes morph and alter, as the situation requires. I do what feels right at the time, even if I know I'd normally disagree with that notion later. I've learned to become flexible.

My open-mindedness had expanded. There was a lot that didn't faze me before, but now that list has grown. I realize that people are just doing what they feel is right, given their background, knowledge base, and influences, same as me. I can see where that limits them in some cases, and see where I can be limiting myself in others. But there you have it. We all do the best we can. I've simply learned to be okay with where I'm at but that it behooves me to try to do better at all times. It helps me to be more accepting of others. Keeps me calm where I maybe would've flared up over someone's bullshit in the past.

This newer attitude of mine just has me wanting to learn from everything around me, at all times. It goes from pleasant to amusing to exhilarating for me to learn something new, depending on how big of a discovery it is. I love this way of thinking!

One thing that's changed is my focus. Mania can make you care about absolutely everything wrong with the world and give you the energy to want to fight it all, to rail against the winds. Thankfully, that passed but I'm left with my sympathy and more so for me, my empathy. I still care but I direct it at only the areas in which my strengths lie. This is why I can't tolerate political discussions. They go nowhere fast and stir up too many bad emotions with nothing productive coming out the other side. Do I have opinions? Sure! Strong ones I don't dare share with just anyone. But will bringing them in the open, on all topics, do me any good? Nope. I prefer to do as Benjamin Franklin suggested way back. Speak less, listen more, don't always try to be right, keep my counsel to myself unless it's asked for.

One thing I've learned above all else: **Everything always changes.** It's the only constant in life. Common sense sort of rides steady over the years, but that's about it. I've learned to not exactly go with the flow but to be adaptable so as to achieve what I need to. It's much less stressful this way.

I've drawn a higher quality of help into my life. Just by pursuing my dream, I have drawn people to me that never would've looked my way in the past. Or, I would not have known I needed them or that I should be looking for them. It goes both ways. Good people see something in me and they want to help, and I know better than ever what a good person looks like, so I know whom to ask for help.

I know how to approach them in a way I never did. I'm clearer on what I want. I even get help in figuring out what I want when I only understand one part of it! I'll have an idea but I need their life experience and practical knowledge to help me turn it into a plan.

I lacked confidence, focus, or proper sense about so much. As I hone these skills to bring me what I need, others on the same path appear. **It's the path that's changed for me.** And now I have a circle of growing friends that is of a quality that makes my life more enjoyable and profitable. They open my eyes to what is possible.

Which brings us to the final point. My life was doomed, over. All hope had been lost; all joy extinguished. My daily existence was one of enduring my symptom load and wondering how it would all end and when. I couldn't see beyond my own suffering. I wasn't aware of anything but my own suffering. I was of no use to anyone and really, was a big negative, a deficit, a burden, to myself and to all who were close to me. Life was pointless and pain-filled.

Now? Life is **purpose driven, laughter-packed,** and **full of possibilities** to the point that I can hardly keep up. My family enjoys me, strangers like me, and my list of friends grows. I'm healthy, strong, of use to others, and I hold a key to this way of life so desperately needed by those who are as I was. I do good things, I feel good, I think better. I'm responsible again, I go out of my way to make life better for everyone I talk or write to, no matter why we're conversing, and I have hope.

I promise you—if you can follow my system, as I have laid it out, you can have hope again, too.

DON'T GO ANYWHERE JUST YET!

If you like what I offered here or start using my system and gain good results, I would love a testimonial from you that I could post on my site. Please email me with your success stories or comments on why you enjoyed the book. This helps others find the same good news, help, or enjoyment you did:

mailto:ken@ittakesgutstobeme.com

And remember, you are now entitled to a one-hour, free consultation with me should you desire it. Now that you know what I'm all about and understand my system, we can talk about your situation and see how best to implement what I've shared.

Please contact me via email and we'll set up a time:

mailto:ken@ittakesgutstobeme.com

I can also speak with your group, participate in your teleseminar, or make myself available for interviews in any media setting.

I appreciate all feedback, good or bad, as it all helps me to shape my material in a way to help the most people. Please email me with your thoughts on my book.

I continually update all of my material and the links to it all can be found at my info site:

www.ittakesgutstobeme.com/blog

I offer as many helpful tips there as is possible, and shed a little more light on my life, both past and present.

I intend to give you all hope! Take care!

Ken

Made in the USA